Mag or Min
Which Are You?

Mag or Min

Which Are You?

Two Patterns of Decision-making That Make You Who You Are

Thomas J. Schur

A Handbook for Change

Website: www.tschur.com

Cover design by Colin G. Schur

Cover photo by Alejandro Garcia

ISBN 978-1-5088-9420-9

First Edition: April 2015

10 9 8 7 6 5 4 3 2 1

To my sons

Colin and Trevor

To their generation and the ones that follow

Table of Contents

List of Figures

As a teenager I was depressed, but did well in school, all the way through two master's degrees, eventually becoming a family therapist. I got married and became a successful therapist, but with a lot of anger that surfaced occasionally in my family relationships. Life got better personally and professionally when I discovered systems theory through the family therapy model of Murray Bowen. This model of therapy has a person work to understand the patterns in their family and how they are caught in them, to the point that the patterns continue to determine how a person lives life in the present day. This work often involves using the family tree as a tool to provide a perspective of these patterns on the larger scale of the extended family. With this understanding, the person goes back to family members and interacts directly, but working to act differently from the old patterns. Over a period of time, as one gets some control to not yield to this old structure of family dynamics, it becomes easier to control oneself in current interactions with nuclear family members, colleagues, friends, neighbors, and so forth. I did this work in my own life over a period of three or four years, and found myself no longer depressed.

My therapy career continued to be successful. I also taught in a major university as an adjunct faculty member, and found I was good at that as well. However, in my career as a therapist and teacher, as well as in my personal life, there was still a constant routine of self-sabotage with remnants of the old anger. Then my life changed significantly when I came up with this idea of magnifying and minifying, and developed it into a framework.

I realized that my modus operandi had always been to operate from the Minification side. This meant that all through my life I had undercut my potential because of how much it scared me. What I did not realize at the time was that in doing my family-of-origin work, I was actually experimenting with controlling my pattern of Minification as I took charge and engaged my family, with whom I had been passive and withdrawn. It is now a different world for me, as I have made major changes in my family relationships, and can capitalize on those gains with this framework of Magnification/Minification, to stay as strong as I can, as a parent, husband, therapist, and teacher. What is this powerful idea?

Magnification and Minification demarcate two different and opposite patterns of decision-making that define who people are. (And "Minify" (Oxford English Dictionnary, 2010) is indeed a real word, simply the opposite of "Magnify.") Those decisions are based on an assessment of the probability of a favorable or unfavorable outcome, and they become patterns that are deeply embedded in how we think and how we act. They become recognizable to ourselves and to others. Over time our behaviors become predictable because the pattern seems to determine the outcome of our decisions. People often experience this situation as not being able to learn from their mistakes. They keep making the same kinds of decisions over and over. However the pattern can change, and this book provides a way to understand it and control its influence in one's life. Using the framework in this book as a guide, a person can gain this self-control by changing how they make decisions, which changes who they are, and then the old pattern is just "not me" anymore.

Magnifiers will make decisions based on the assumption that any task to be attempted will almost always work out, despite the odds against it. They "magnify" the possibility of a favorable outcome and "minify" the probability of an unfavorable outcome. Minifiers will make decisions based on the assumption that any task to be attempted will seldom work out, despite the odds in favor of it. They "minify" the possibility of a favorable outcome and "magnify" the probability of an unfavorable outcome.

This book explains the two patterns and how you can change them to change your Self, through decision-making. As you will see, I have created a continuum for this framework with Magnification on one side and Minification on the other. These are the extremes on either side of the Middle. A person has a Home position on one side or the other, which identifies the stable point for the Self. Changing the pattern of decision-making to be more functional in life changes the Home position to a point closer to the Middle. This book makes extensive use of this continuum in the charts throughout.

This is a powerful idea and a substantial and practical framework to implement it. What can account for the power of this idea? Here are some of the factors.

1. How intuitive the idea is

People get it right away. Even if they are initially confused about which side they operate from, they know this is important and could be very useful once they figure it out.

2. The pure simplicity of it

People at their core operate in either the Magnifier or Minifier mode, and they never change from one side to the other, even if they think they do. They live their entire lives from one side of the continuum or the other. Change is very possible and can be very powerful, but the change is to move closer to the Middle on the continuum, never to the other side. Once this is understood, a person no longer has to figure out which way the Middle is. This understanding eliminates an enormous amount of doubting oneself and one's decisions.

3. Practicality: the constant opportunity to practice getting better

We are constantly making decisions. Each decision, big or little, daily or once-in-a-lifetime, provides a way to experiment with moving toward the Middle on the continuum.

4. Reliability

The results of the personal experiments are so reliable. Once people have identified the Home position of the Self on the continuum, they are able to recognize quickly and accurately when they are defaulting to the old pattern of Magnification or Minification, and when they are working more toward the middle.

5. Productivity: the depth of change possible

By changing the pattern of decision-making, a person changes the Self, and this change leverages changes in the systems people operate in, be it their family, their job, or their social networks.

6. Sound theoretical foundation

This is not just another self-help technique whose effectiveness can only be explained by the testaments of certain people for whom it works. This framework certainly has that kind of corroboration, but more importantly, it is based in a set of integrated theories that explain why it works and why it is so powerful. This will be presented in various parts of the book, and as a whole in the Appendix for those readers interested in the theoretical foundation itself.

I am a therapist and a teacher. Over the past 40 years I have made major changes in my Self that have changed my life in significant ways. Thirty years ago I did the primary work of returning to my family of origin and engaging them face-to-face as I worked to change the old patterns by holding my positions and dealing with the anxiety that that process generated. Only after I discovered Mag/Min and had done this work did I realize I could understand my work *in terms of* Mag/Min. Now I build on that foundation by explicitly using Mag/Min in my current life with my nuclear and extended families, clients, supervisees, students, colleagues, and friends.

In addition to my experience with my own changes, this framework has been field tested in other important ways. Over the past 10 years I have witnessed major changes in the lives of my clients, students, and supervisees using this framework. Also, in response to a recent inquiry, my colleagues told me that they use the Mag/Min framework as they work with their clients, using it to understand and help them, but also formally teaching them the framework as well as explaining it to other colleagues. And, they were very clear that they use the framework explicitly in their personal lives.

Another way it has been tested is in the initial response of people generally as I present it in classes and other forums and as people read it on my website. Most often they grasp the basic idea quickly and are frequently excited about the idea of these two patterns of decision-making. As they explore it more, they may question it and have disagreements, but the initial understanding remains intact. I would add that this initial and very common response of understanding indicates the viability of testing it further in a more formal way through scientific research.

I have said many times over the course of writing this book that I was writing it for my children. I have seen it clearly as part of a legacy for my own family, but at the same time as a product of my career that makes a contribution for the betterment of the world.

As people make changes in themselves their relationships change, from the small, intimate ones of the family to larger societal ones. I have made significant personal changes resulting in better relationships with my wife, my children and other family members, and now hope to leverage this change of Self into changes at a larger level by publishing this book. That is why I have worked hard to make the writing personal, so that the reader gets a sense of me as the person who has developed these ideas which have a universality that can be accessible for many people, who can use them to make changes in themselves, in their close relationships, and in larger networks. So it is a self-improvement book that goes well beyond one person.

But what do I think makes for a good self-improvement book? First, it must not be shallow or gimmicky. It must not seem like an entrepreneurial effort to make money, making outrageous claims that sound too good to be true. Second, the author must be real. I need to have a sense of the person of the writer, where they have a presence in the writing. This usually means that the content comes from their own experience that they decided to write about, not from a project they decided to market. Third, the book must be based in a credible framework that is broad and deep, in contrast to one idea with a lot of tips. The foundation for the framework must be robust, so that it can be scrutinized and challenged, like the science behind a nutrition book or the psychology behind a book on dealing with trauma.

How-to-live-life-better books that do not meet these criteria make me feel like I have to give up something to read them, which makes it difficult to trust what I am reading. It is not the sense of letting go of something that is bad for me, but of being sold something that is being advertised. The product may sound intriguing and useful, but I have a nagging sense of being sold something for someone else's gain.

So now I have written one of these books. How well does it meet my own criteria? Actually, I was able to articulate the criteria only after I had finished it. Now having created what I think is a good book, I realize that these criteria serve to explain why it is good. Here is how I see my book fares with these criteria.

First: I have been careful in the book, as I am in my therapy practice with my clients, not to make unrealistic claims about how this framework can change people's lives, but without discounting the power of the idea.

Second: this book is very personal for me. I have presented my autobiography with specific details and charts for the reader to be able to understand the concepts of Magnification and Minification. Also, in order to explain the framework I have used many examples throughout which come directly from experiences in my own life, as well as with my clients, students and supervisees. And, I have dedicated the book to my sons.

Third: the foundation for the book provides a broad perspective as it rests on the work of several important people in different fields: a psychiatrist who developed a major theory of family therapy; an anthropologist who developed a seminal idea about identity and existential anxiety, and a biologist who developed a radical new theory of language. In addition to this comprehensive foundation is the perspective of the book itself, which is indeed broad and deep as it is about life and death—survival.

Acknowledgements

This book has been a long time in the making. It has been a process of working with the ideas with my students, my clients, my supervisees, my colleagues, and my family, as the integration developed over a period of 10 years or more and has come to fruition in this book. There have been many people who have been on this journey with me and without whom that integration and this book would never have happened. Some have been with me from the beginning and some have joined me more recently. Others, like my previous students and clients, have been an important part of it, but are no longer in contact with me. And one in particular has not been in my life for a long time, but is always in my thoughts, because she died in 1985, Margaret York.

It was Margaret who introduced this young therapist to the ideas of Murray Bowen, and shaped my career as she taught me about systems and how to have a deep respect for clients and their pain.

Over the years up to the present, generations of students in the School of Social Work at Syracuse University gave me the opportunity to try out my ideas in my classes. They accepted my challenge to think systems and then to write a "Becker paper." In these papers they shared deeply personal life stories as they described their denial systems that protected them from existential anxiety. Presenting Ernest Becker's book *Denial of Death* in class, answering their questions, and then grading their papers forced me to understand Becker's seminal idea of denial. It was like a constant workout with these ideas. As you will see, Becker's ideas are a major foundation for this book along with those of Bowen.

The network of colleagues that comprise the Next Generation/Singers group in Syracuse, New York has been invaluable in my exploring and understanding these ideas. Their love for me and each other has created a community that has made learning and self-development possible for all of us, and for me at a depth that has enabled me to trust myself as a leader and a thinker competent enough to write this book.

Many of my clients don't realize how important their work in therapy has been for my understanding of the processes of human change. Many times I have said things to them with a great deal of confidence, but knew that I had no idea of how I knew it. I now know I learned it from them over the years. Magnify/Minify was one of those ideas.

My supervisees, both Social Workers and Marriage and Family Therapists, both young and seasoned, provided a different forum for the development of these ideas. From them I also learned about the process of human change, but here the unique opportunity was to learn from their work with their clients about the process of therapy itself and how people change. I learned about what goes on with the therapist and their own changes as they work with their clients. Increasingly, Mag/Min became an essential tool, as we would figure out whether the therapist was a Magnifier or Minifier and whether the clients were Mags or Mins.

In this regard, I am especially grateful to my recent classes in the Marriage and Family Therapy Program at Syracuse University who helped me deepen my understanding of my own framework. And from my supervision of many of them, I learned about their personal development as well as my own, as they became better therapists and I became a more accomplished supervisor.

Then there are specific people who have made important and identifiable contributions to me in the writing of this book. Aimee Delman has understood these ideas from the very beginning of my putting them together. She read some of my early writings about what I called back then "Potential/Limitation," and gave me advice I have used over and over in writing the book. She told me to be strong and make my claims about what I thought; to speak from my own experience and write from a personal voice.

Bobbi Schnorr also has understood these ideas well for a long time and, with that understanding, read a much later draft when the book was organized into chapters, but still incomplete. Her editing was very valuable at that stage to format the book for the final organization.

Paul Hughes has worked with me (frequently on the golf course) in the development of the idea that is near and dear to him, language and existential anxiety. He continues to remind me of the critical importance of this part as a foundation for Mag/Min.

My friend Bob Kawa helped me understand the dynamics of Magnification outside the realm of my professional world, again on the golf course.

Then there is my family. My son Colin certainly heard these ideas before he left home, but that was as a teenager and young adult. Then he became a graphic designer, and contributed to this project by creating the cover and by providing consistent and reliable consultation on the overall formatting of the book, which has been invaluable.

My son Trevor had also heard these ideas growing up, but has contributed more recently by working with me to understand himself and his friends. This has been very helpful for me as I have been able to test out the validity of this framework with my own flesh and blood.

Diana, my wife, has been an important part of this book, just by living with me and hearing about these ideas many times over and in many iterations, as they would develop and change over the years. While she has read various drafts of the text and made suggestions that have prompted me to make some major changes, her most valuable contribution has been the continual discussions about how she uses the framework in her personal and business relationships. This has kept the ideas constantly present for me as we live them together.

Lois Gridley, my copy editor, has kept my copy clean, an expected but critical contribution. She and I have worked well together, using "old-fashioned" hardcopy as well as digital tracking. In addition, she has provided consistent and reliable support for the project, often providing important and helpful resources from her own professional network.

Introduction

"No problem."

"I never worry about details."

"Go for it!"

"What do you have to lose?"

"Sure I can."

"That never works."

"Must allow for complications."

"I'll have to think about that."

"That could be dangerous."

"I could never do that."

The Framework

Everyone has a Self, and that Self is essential for managing a person's anxiety about survival as they go about their lives each day. How effective the Self is in managing this anxiety can be observed in a person's pattern of decision-making. The degree of functionality of this pattern can be designated on a continuum. The continuum is constructed with Magnification on one end, Minification on the other, and a Middle which signifies the highest level of functioning. The "Home position" for a person identifies which reflex the person has, Mag or Min, with that point being on one side or the other of the Middle, and then to what extent responses to the reflex allow for good assessments as the basis for decisions, indicated by how far its position is away from the midpoint. A good assessment is one that does not distort the possibility of a favorable outcome. The extreme ends reflect patterns of lower functioning with poorer assessments, while points closer to the Middle reflect better decisions and higher functioning. The Home position represents the stable, though not necessarily high functioning, overall pattern of decision-making.

The reflex is a perceptual reflex that occurs when a person is challenged to make a decision in which there is a distinct focus on one possible outcome to the exclusion of others. At the extremes, the Magnifier's perception excludes the possibility of an unfavorable outcome and the Minifier's perception excludes the possibility of a favorable outcome. Better decisions are those based on a balanced assessment of the possibility of the outcome being favorable or unfavorable, which requires managing the response to the reflex.

It is important to understand that this reflex is based on a perception that always recognizes both possibilities of a favorable and an unfavorable outcome. The difference between the Magnifier's perception and the Minifier's is simply which one stands out, while the other remains in the background. For the Magnifier, the favorable stands out, while the unfavorable is present but in the background. For the Minifier, the unfavorable stands out, while the favorable is present but in the background.

A person can change their pattern of decision-making, either Mag or Min, by managing this reflex so decisions are not as automatic as they maintain the pattern over and over. In this way the Self changes and so does the level of functioning. On the continuum, this would be reflected in movement of the Home position to a point closer to the Middle.

The image of a continuum with Mag on one side and Min on the other, has always been present in my mind as I have worked and reworked the complex ideas that form the whole of the framework. It captures the basic assumption that the process of magnification and minification is *one* dynamic with two different and opposite modes. This simple diagram of the continuum led to the development of the many charts in the book. The charts and the ideas fed each other. I would find that a concept could be described by drawing it out as a chart, and then that chart would lead to others, and through those modifications I would discover new understandings of the ideas. In the end I realized how important the charts have been for me as part of this reciprocal process of writing and understanding. I have incorporated these charts extensively into the book, based on the assumption that it will also help the reader to have the graphic images to illustrate the ideas.

There are three main components of the fully developed charts: the two ends of the continuum, the Middle, and the three dimensional sides that extend the continuum through time. The graphic on the cover, which represents all of these elements, serves as an iconic portrayal of the framework.

Figure 0.1 depicts the basic continuum and is a good way to begin to grasp this framework, as it displays the first two elements just described, the ends and the Middle, in a two-dimensional chart. It is the first in the series of diagrams that will be presented throughout this book, with later ones developed to incorporate the third dimension of time, which help the reader understand the depth and complexity of this powerful framework.

Decision-making Characteristics

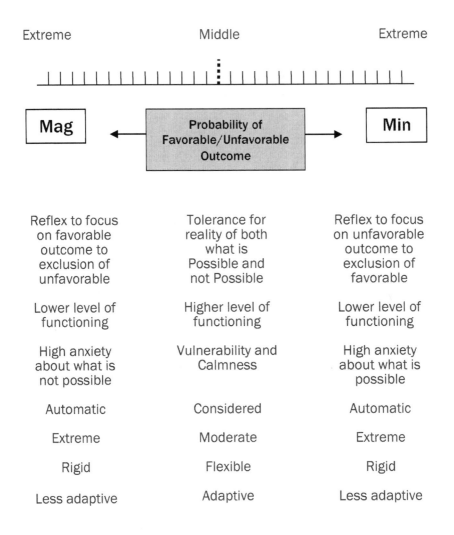

Figure 0.1

Clarifications — What it is and what it is not

About change

So this book is about change. It is about working to change the patterns of one's decision-making to change the Basic self, and thereby one's ability to live life more fully. It is not about simply helping people make better practical decisions. The work of changing the patterns of decision-making changes people at a much deeper level, and in so doing, it changes their relationships with others.

Not mainstream

This idea of Magnification/Minification as a continuum of extremes runs counter to a strong assumption of Western cultures that prefers magnification to minification and does not see magnification as extreme. No one strives to achieve only limited goals. Excellence lies in the highest achievements, not in limited ones. People feel good about being rewarded for their efforts to do their very best, not with results from attempts to just do what they can. The common assumption is that always striving for the highest goals, even unrealistic ones, will yield better results than settling for less.

This Magnification/Minification framework makes a very different assumption. It rejects the notion that a person always has to strive for the best, seeing that approach as too limiting, too restrictive, because it closes out the option of accepting limitation when it is the most productive choice. This is not at all to say that this approach values minification over magnification. It values the Middle, the area of highest functioning. However, the point here is to clarify and counter the cultural bias toward unlimited potential. The Basic self functioning from magnification can be just as dysfunctional, when functioning from the extreme of minification.

The following are a few examples of what I mean by operating from the extreme of magnification: continuing to do physical workouts when tired, risking injury; continually pushing a child to excel in academics, or sports, to the exclusion of rest, sleep, and quiet time; demanding that employees work overtime regularly to grow the business, eroding morale; committing oneself to so many volunteer activities that one has to cancel frequently and then incurs a reputation of being unreliable.

This way of living is less functional because the person has less control of their life. External events set the limits, not the person themselves. There is a drive to excel with a constant anxiety about failure. There is less self-regulation.

The extreme of Minification is just as dysfunctional, but it is more easily recognized by the Western culture than the dysfunction of extreme Magnification. People understand that a person who withdraws from their responsibilities as a parent or an employee, complaining that it is just too difficult to discipline their children or do the job their boss expects, has a problem. But this is the same problem of self-regulation as the Magnifier, because the person lets external circumstances such as the reactions of their boss or their children determine their functioning. Higher functioning for both is toward the Middle.

This is not to say that working toward the Middle is giving in to the easy way. Far from it. It is a major challenge for the person operating from Magnification to allow more limitations and magnify less (just as for the person from Minification to allow more potential and minify less). The Mag/Min framework shifts the challenge from pushing to the extreme, where there is less self-regulation, to the Middle, where the person has to exert self-control and discipline to not yield to giving in to magnification (or minification). The reward for this major effort is more calmness, better judgment, and more productivity in the long run.

Not about optimism/pessimism

How do the attitudes of optimism and pessimism relate to these ideas? The Oxford English Dictionary defines "optimism" as: "Hopefulness and confidence about the future or the successful outcome of something; a tendency to take a favourable or hopeful view" (Oxford English Dictionnary, 2010). This is contrasted with its opposite "pessimism," defined as: "The tendency or disposition to look at the worst aspect of things; the attitude or habit of taking a negative view of circumstances, the future" (Oxford English Dictionnary, 2010). Generally people do not find pessimism appealing. From common experience, confirmed by these definitions, one can predict that there would be a cultural bias toward magnification and against minification from the valuing of Optimism over Pessimism.

For this reason, it is inaccurate and confusing to equate the Mag/Min continuum with the Optimism–Pessimism polarity. Mag/Min is a continuum of the Basic self, going from either one of the two extremes on either end, toward a range in the middle, with people falling at various points all along that continuum. Optimism and pessimism are generally viewed as opposites, with no real consideration of a middle position, certainly not one that is valued. Clearly for the Mag/Min framework, the "best" is in the middle and the "worst" is out on the two extremes.

Not about positive/negative self-concept

The notion of self-concept is obviously about the Self, about how one sees oneself. However, the framework of Magnification/Minification is not congruent with this notion of a positive or negative self-concept, for the same reason that the polarity of Optimism and Pessimism does not fit, namely, because of the assumption that a positive self-concept is better than a negative self-concept. Mag/Min is an alternative framework that allows for a realistic acceptance of

Self, instead of evaluating Self as positive or negative.

From Minification, a person would distort one's view of Self by downplaying their strengths, and that could be called a negative self-concept. To "improve" that self-concept, the person would be encouraged to value themselves more, emphasizing and valuing their strengths. But that is an unbalanced approach, as it distorts the actual weaknesses and may emphasize strengths that are not that strong. On the other side, from Magnification, the person values their strengths and calls that a positive self-concept because a focus on strength is valued. How real those strengths may be is questionable, because that is the automatic reaction of the response of Magnification. At the same time, any assessment of actual weaknesses is not allowed, because it would diminish the valued positive self-concept.

On the Magnification/Minification continuum, the best functioning is in the middle, between either extreme. In regard to positive and negative self-concept, the best assessment of Self is one of acceptance. It consists of an accurate appraisal of one's strengths and weaknesses. This Middle position is more mature, as it is more adaptive, because one can better respond to challenges with the knowledge of what actual strengths one possesses to deal with the challenge, and what actual weaknesses prevent an effective response to the challenge.

That is why it does not make sense to talk of changing an attitude to being less of an optimist or less of a pessimist, or to have a better self-concept. On the other hand, it does make sense to take action through decisions that are based on positions of less extreme Magnification or less extreme Minification. So working toward the Middle will refer to a direction of action, not to changing an attitude.

The Middle position can be confusing, and becomes a serious problem when a person is over-extended in her daily responsibilities and knows she needs to cut back to have a better life. Initially, this seems to her to be choosing the lesser, second-best option, but not the best as I contend. This shift is difficult for her as she is tempted to override limits. This middle-ground confusion is also a problem for people who limit themselves too much. For another person, choosing to act on his strengths seems reasonable to him initially, but becomes disturbing when he realizes that he will actually be tempted to sabotage his owns efforts if he chooses to be successful.

In spite of this counter-intuitive confusion, it does make sense for the woman above to figure out ways to not always act on her need to overachieve and take unnecessary risks, creating daily stress. This relief can lead to higher levels of productivity. It also makes sense for the man above to discover how he can take the initiative on tasks in his life and not continually minimize his productivity, always with the stress of being overwhelmed. Both of them can experiment with specific ways to magnify less or minify less, which moves them toward the Middle on the continuum.

These changes can have a major impact on how they live their lives. People making these changes tell me repeatedly that something is the same, but something is very different. As they explain it, what they mean is that they do not feel like they are a different person, but that their life has changed enormously.

Work

It is very important to clarify here that a person does not just adopt the Middle position. One can only get to the Middle by working from one of the ends of the continuum of Magnification or Minification. Everyone has a Home position on one side or the other, and the possibilities for change require the work of focusing on oneself, and experimenting with changing the old, dysfunctional patterns of behavior based on too much magnification or too much minification.

People operating from Magnification need to work to allow more limitation in their lives, controlling automatic responses of always taking on the "challenges" to be a better parent, be more successful in their jobs, become more physically fit, and so forth, disregarding the risk or costs. People operating from Minification need to work to allow more possibilities, controlling the automatic responses to be "realistic" and accepting of life with parenting, work, health, and so forth, disregarding the actual likelihood of success.

A note to the reader is in order here. Precisely because of the basic human tendency to focus on the other when faced with the unknown and possible threat to the Self, people from one side of the continuum are often highly reactive to people from the other side. As you consider these ideas and apply them to yourself, you may well have strong reactions about the other side. Magnifiers have trouble understanding others who do not have the initiative to take charge in life, and Minifiers cannot stand others who refuse to slow down and be more realistic. The other side generates precisely the anxiety one's Home position protects one from. Hence it is important to stay grounded in Self, trusting one's own experience and understanding of one's patterns and not be distracted by a focus on the patterns of others, even in reading this book!

When focused on Self, people from each end of the Magnification/Minification continuum know what they need to do, but are afraid to do it. The over functioning parent knows she needs to stop trying so hard, but is afraid if she stops, everything will fall apart. The perpetual student knows he has to get out in the world and use what he has learned, but is afraid he does not know enough and will fail. The real challenge of this approach is that each person needs to take action to control the magnification or minification, depending on which end they start from, and then tolerate the anxiety of doing that. They both need to trust the current forces in their life that press them in the direction of more magnification or more minification, and allow the anxiety. That anxiety really never goes away, but people learn over time to trust it as part of a process of being more themselves as they change and become more effective in their lives.

Why is it so hard?

Because of the anxiety. It is important to understand the meaning of anxiety in this book. People certainly recognize anxiety as they experience it in their lives. They would generally describe it as a feeling of worry or concern, but one that ranges widely from terror, as when one's life is threatened, to a mild concern that they may have said the wrong thing. This book takes the perspective that anxiety is simply a fact of life and is always present to one degree or another. Anxiety is not something to be gotten rid of like a disease, but something to be managed daily and throughout one's life. Of course, this certainly does not mean one is always aware of being anxious. Usually not. People generally are not aware of being anxious until something happens that triggers that realization.

A fundamental assumption of this book is that this anxiety is being managed all the time, *especially when one is not aware of it*, and that this lack of awareness is a crucial part of how it is managed. The mind works to protect a person from the experience of being vulnerable, becoming anxious about every threat, and then not being able to function effectively in daily life. In this book this process will be referred to as "denial" which is not a dysfunctional rejection of reality, but a functional protection from debilitating anxiety. Obviously, at times people become aware of being anxious, and sometimes that is very functional and sometimes it is not. It is functional when there is a clear threat, as when one's life is in danger, or when one has said something that does indeed offend another. However, this protective mechanism of denial is not functional when one distorts the threat of physical danger or the fear of having said something offensive. Distorted perceptions lead to poor decisions about how to respond to a situation.

Even more importantly, continued distortions that function as protective denial can lead to a pattern of decision-making that ends up organizing one's life, because the pattern becomes a way to manage anxiety. In addition, because it becomes habitual, the person is not aware of how it is actually protecting them from the ever-present anxiety of simply being in the world and surviving. This book will argue that this pattern of decision-making is so pervasive and powerful that it comes to define who a person is, and that the pattern can be understood in the very simple terms of Magnification or Minification. At the extreme ends of the continuum the pattern becomes more rigid and there is less ability to adapt to life events as they come up.

Now back to the question of why change is so hard. To experiment with changing one's pattern of decision-making, to experiment with one's pattern of Magnification or Minification, is to experiment with changing one's mechanism for managing their anxiety about being in the world. To experiment with this protection brings the awareness of that anxiety to the surface. The person is then experimenting with an important mechanism of protection, identified here as denial. This protection mechanism is powerful and not easy to change because it is so important for people's functioning as they make decisions every day. To change the pattern is difficult work.

However, the reward for this change is relief from the hyper-vigilant focus on the threat of too much limitation for the Magnifier and too much potential for the Minifier, and the calmness in the Middle of an acceptance of life with all its ups and downs. With this acceptance comes better decisions that lead to more adaptive behaviors in the face of life stressors (Refer back to Figure 0.1).

Decision-making and the process of
Magnification and Minification

Magnification or Minification is a perceptual reflex that occurs when a person is faced with a situation that challenges the status quo. The brain of the person with the Mag reflex immediately focuses on how this challenge can turn out well, and the brain of the person with the

Min reflex immediately focuses on how the situation may not turn out well. The reflex is a perception in which the possibility of a favorable outcome or an unfavorable outcome stands out in the foreground, with the opposite possibility (unfavorable for Mag and favorable for Min) remaining in the background. It is important to note that this is an instant *perception* about how the action to be taken in response to the challenge will turn out. It is not necessarily a good assessment of the actual probability of a favorable or unfavorable outcome.

My experience in working with this framework is that people do not have control over this reflex. It is an immediate perception one way or the other. Decision-making comes in at the point when a person becomes aware of the situation and the challenge, and has a choice about how to respond to it. The basis of this framework is that over time these choices fall into a pattern, and that this pattern becomes a major, defining characteristic of the Self of a person. Again it is important to note that this pattern is a pattern of the perception and the actions that follow. *It is not a pattern of whether the actual outcomes are successful or not.*

A person with the Mag reflex has the automatic reflex to focus on how the challenge can be overcome, and then makes decisions to make that happen. He or she is not focused on factors that may not be able to be overcome, or aware of the consequences of the decisions that may make the situation worse. Those factors remain in the background as this person repeats this pattern in response to the Mag/Min reflex over and over, stabilizing major components of the person's identity, so that he or she can recognize it as describing their Self.

A person with the Min reflex has the automatic reflex to focus on how daunting the challenge is, and then makes decisions to minimize the dangers, not focused on factors that may actually be strengths and resources to succeed with the challenge, nor aware of the consequences of the decisions that may make the situation better.

Those factors remain in the background as this person repeats this pattern in response to the Mag/Min reflex over and over, stabilizing major components of the person's identity, so that he or she can recognize it as describing their Self.

For both then, the Self is stabilized, but with the Home position on different sides of the continuum (either Mag or Min), and with that Home position ranging from the extreme end to the more moderate Middle range.

It is important to note that this is a reflex that happens instantly, without much thought. In the Mag/Min reflex, the foreground focus is on the possibilities of a favorable outcome for the Magnifier and on the possibilities of an unfavorable outcome for the Minifier. Also note that in the process of perception there are always the two elements of foreground and background that form a whole, but the reflex in the brain "selects" only one. The basis for conceptualizing the Mag/Min reflex in this way comes from the notion of figure/ground from the field of Gestalt psychology.

Gestalt is a theory of perception that was developed in the early part of the 20th century in Germany (Kohler, 1947) with the conceptualization that a perception needs to be understood as a whole. One of the major concepts in that theory is figure/ground, which has been popularized in the famous graphic of Rubin's vase (Pind, 2013) and can be found in many psychology books.

In this illustration, one sees either a vase or two faces, depending on which element of the image is figure and which is ground. Both elements are always present and are background for the other, depending on which one the brain selects as figural. The figure/ground dynamic is also found currently in many fields of design.

In my framework, Mag/Min is a whole perception of the possible outcome of a decision. Both possibilities are always present, but one stands out more than the other, and more so the farther the Home position is from the Middle. The outcome is either favorable or unfavorable. It works out or it does not. For the Magnifier the possibility of a favorable outcome is figural while the unfavorable one is still present but as ground. For the Minifier the unfavorable outcome stands out, while the possibility of a favorable outcome remains in the background. Using Gestalt's figure/ground concept, one could say that the closer the Home position is to the Middle, the more the person from either side of the continuum can allow the ground element to come into the foreground. The Magnifier can allow the perception of an unfavorable outcome to be considered as a possibility along with the favorable one, and the Minifier can allow the perception of a favorable outcome as a possibility along with the unfavorable one.

I suggest that Mag/Min is a reflex because I posit that it is an instinctual, primitive process in the brain akin to the fight/flight response. Fight/flight is the idea developed by Walter Cannon (Cannon, 1932) that there is a physiological reaction in the body of animals in response to an immediate threat that prepares their bodies for the action of fighting or fleeing. My contention is that the brain uses the same mechanism to protect the Self, which I hypothesize is essential for the survival of the person. In this view, Magnification is the equivalent of the fight response and Minification of the flight response. I suggest that this survival mechanism operates at this same level of anxiety and threat.

There is an important link here of fight/flight with the Gestalt concept of figure/ground that pertains to Mag/Min. My hypothesis is that a person develops a survival reflex in which the fight option is figural, magnifying the likelihood of winning the fight. Or they develop the survival reflex in which the flight option is figural, minifying the likelihood of winning the fight. At the extremes of *either* Mag or Min, the odds of actually surviving over the long term are lower, because the Magnifier will always fight regardless of the chances for success, and the Minifier will always flee regardless of the chances for success. Closer to the Middle, the Mag allows the possibility of fleeing to become figural and considers it as a viable option for survival. Similarly, the Min allows the possibility of fighting to become figural and considers it as a viable option for survival.

This hypothesis of Mag/Min as a physiological reflex that protects the Self at the same level of anxiety as the physical threat for an animal is, of course, a large leap. But it is a legitimate one based on Bowen's Natural Systems theory of the family, and my experience in working with this framework of Magnification/Minification. Bowen theory is a major foundation for this whole Mag/Min framework. Seminal concepts of the theory will be explained throughout the book as they are pertinent. For now Michael Kerr's brief description (Kerr & Bowen, 1988) will suffice: "Family systems theory is based on the assumptions that the human is a product of evolution and that human behavior is significantly regulated by the same natural processes that regulate the behavior of all other living things" (p. 3).

While it is axiomatic that everyone operates from one side or the other of the continuum, how far out from the Middle on whichever side the Home position or self-stabilizing point is, does make a difference, because it affects the process of making decisions. Basically, the farther out from the Middle on the Magnification/Minification continuum one operates, the narrower the range of choices a person has available to respond to the reflex of Mag or Min in making decisions that stabilize the Self. This is because the responses to the reflex are immediate. Closer to the Middle, the range of choices is wider, as there is an interval in which a person takes the time, which may be very brief or very long depending on the situation, to consider different options. Nonetheless, my firm contention is that one always has choices, and a person can change the Self through changing the pattern of decision-making, regardless of how far out one's Home position is from the Middle on the continuum.

Here's how it works. Every day people make little decisions, like what to eat for dinner, whether to discipline one's child, or when to go to sleep. In some places in the world those decisions might be about how to get food for that day, how to protect one's child from violence, or whether one can risk sleep at all that night. Nonetheless, these are small, daily decisions. They are small because they occur frequently and do not have an immediately apparent long-term effect. One can also talk about big decisions that one does not make every day and that do seem to have large consequences. In this category might be such decisions as whether to go off to war, have another baby, try an experimental drug, change careers, leave one's spouse, and so forth.

Sometimes little decisions do have big impacts, like buying a winning lottery ticket, or changing lanes on the Interstate and having an accident. The opposite, big decisions with little impact, can also happen, as one leaves his third wife and finds his life no different really, or discovering that bariatric surgery did not result in long-term weight loss without lifestyle changes.

This book is based on the idea that change happens through changing one's process of decision-making. But how does one distinguish what decisions are important and lead to changes in one's life? This is where the systems foundation for this framework of Magnification/Minification makes it so powerful.

A basic premise of systems theory is that one can understand how a system operates if one can recognize its patterns which reflect its stabilizing process. The decisions a person makes in their life, both big and little, can be understood in terms of patterns that are part of the balance of the system. From this point of view, the significance of a particular decision is not whether it is big or little, but whether it fits the same pattern or not. If it reflects the same pattern as most previous decisions, it can be assumed from systems thinking that the decision maintains the balance of the system, whether the system is a marriage, a family, or an organization. If it is atypical, it has the possibility of deviating from the typical pattern and therefore disrupting the balance of the system and creating change.

One of the major assumptions of this book is that patterns of decision-making can be understood specifically as falling on one side or the other of the Magnification/Minification continuum. People can make little decisions about not choosing to go outside that night because the weather is threatening, or big decisions about not seeking another job because they think they will not get it. Both decisions are consistent with a pattern of operating from Minification. For that person to decide to go out, or go for the job, would be different and could change the balance of their systems if he or she maintained this different pattern over time. From the Mag side, a person could decide to pass a car that is going only a few miles over the speed limit, or stay up all night to prepare a presentation to get an edge on a competitor. Again, these decisions are based in the same pattern, namely of Magnification. For that person to relax and not pass the car or go to bed instead of preparing more, could be part of a major change in their pattern. What is important is whether a particular decision departs from the longstanding, stabilizing pattern and moves toward the Middle, not whether it is big or little.

In the end, this book contends that decision-making gives a person access to the possibility of making major changes in one's life as one becomes aware of one's pattern of deciding, either from Magnification or Minification, and uses this awareness in making decisions to change the pattern and the Self.

Foundation from other major works

This whole framework evolved out of my experience as a therapist and teacher, but is well grounded in the work of others that has been foundational in my development over the years. The basic idea about Magnification and Minification came initially from Ernest Becker's *Denial of Death*. The broader systems theory framework that informs my lifelong work as a therapist and teacher comes from the Natural Systems theory of Murray Bowen. My ideas about language that relate to Magnification and Minification, as well as to my therapy and teaching, come from the work of Humberto Maturana. Neuroscientists whose work supports this framework in various ways are Daniel Siegel, Joseph LeDoux, Terrence Deacon, and Antonio Damasio.

Outline of the Book — What to expect

The book begins with an explanation in Chapter 1 of the process of decision-making in general as a pattern of organizing the Self, and how changing this pattern by making different decisions can change one's life. The chapter will show how the Magnification/Minification continuum provides a specific and practical way to change the pattern.

This chapter also begins to develop a sequence of many diagrams throughout the book that provide the reader with a graphic way to conceptualize the Mag/Min continuum and use it in the work of changing the Self.

With a basic understanding of the Magnification/Minification continuum established, Chapter 2 provides a variety of ways, including many examples, for the reader to identify their Home position as one of either Magnification or Minification. Without knowing one's Home position, the rest of the book will be difficult to understand. This is not to say that the reader cannot begin with a hunch about the Home position, read on, and then come back to Chapter 2 one or more times to confirm or revise that hunch.

With the identification of the Home position established, the next step is to understand what change is about. What is involved in changing the Home position to shift it more toward the Middle? What can one expect from such a move? Is the change process different for a Magnifier than for a Minifier? Why would someone want to do the work of changing the pattern in the first place? Chapter 3 answers these and other questions. This is where the decision-making component becomes specific and practical.

Chapter 4 explains how the dynamics of Magnification and

Minification operate in relationships, using Bowen theory's concept of triangles. It provides examples of how Mag/Min patterns of interaction stabilize relationships and how those patterns can change.

With the Self as such a core concept in this Mag/Min framework, Chapter 5, "The Self as Narrative," presents an explanation of the Self. It defines the Self in terms of language, and explains how the Self operates in human relationship systems with a focus on the critical issue of stability.

With the Self defined in terms of language and the importance of the narrative of the Self, it makes sense to present stories to help the reader further understand this framework. Chapter 6 presents several stories. One is my personal story, my autobiography, along with others that are composites of people I have worked with using this framework. These composites, like other examples throughout the book, are not actual people but rather characters based on real people from my practice, my classes, and my family. Think of them as people in an historical novel, where the elements of history remain strictly factual and consistent as a whole, while the characters bring that actual history to life at the personal level of individual people. In a very similar way, the characters in this book are credible renditions of people that manifest the dynamics of my framework of Magnification/Minification, which remain true to my experience of working with this actual framework with real people. It is a vehicle for making the material more understandable, especially as the reader can identify with those characters. Just as the author of that historical novel understands the actual history so well that he or she can create "real" characters, I understand Mag/Min so well that I can generate a variety of stories based on my experiences with real people that demonstrate the framework.

Chapter 7 condenses the whole procedure of moving from the identification of the Home position through the change process by creating a "Guide" framed in terms of decision-making. While the whole book is a handbook, this chapter serves both as a summary of the framework after the initial reading, as well as a reference for review in the future.

The FAQ (Frequently Asked Questions) section at the end lists a set of questions and answers that have come up over the years as I have presented this framework. Readers will find this section useful to recognize and validate their questions, as well as to gain a better understanding of the approach from specific issues that arise.

Finally, for those interested in exploration of the foundational ideas for this book, the Appendix describes the bodies of work this framework draws from.

C h a p t e r 1

Decisions

Two people: Mary and Paul

Mary

Mary was very competent as a small business entrepreneur. She had set up a specialty restaurant after graduating from high school; it had become very profitable in just a few years of operation and was providing a good income for her family. She was also a very responsible and effective mother of two sons with learning disabilities. However, she had been "burning the candle at both ends," spending many hours micro-managing her business, then coming home and investing a lot of time and energy working with her sons on their homework, and dealing with their school and their teachers to provide a good education for her children. She provided meals for her family, counting on her husband to do some of the cooking, though he often brought home take-out food or took the boys out to eat.

She came to therapy in crisis, depressed because she suddenly could no longer manage it all, and very anxious about that. The therapist told her she needed to stop trying so hard and accept that many of her goals were impossible to accomplish. This suggestion was exactly contrary to her fundamental worldview of always striving to achieve against all odds, which had worked so well for her up until now. When she would present dilemmas about career and parenting decisions, the therapist would talk about saying "no" to business opportunities where she was too responsible, and "no" to doing too much for her children. This effort led to an experience of pain and an awareness of an old helplessness from her childhood, but also to a calmness that was new and surprised her.

She spent a year in therapy, working on controlling her reflex to overcompensate for her fear of failure, both with her children and in her career. Through this experimentation she began to actually trust limitations, as she realized her children were doing better academically and her career was progressing. In a move that was contrary to her old entrepreneurial role, doing all the jobs from menial to executive, she went back to school, enrolling in a college program for hotel management. Now she was the student, where she was able to let the teachers take charge and learn from them.

She was able to manage her school schedule to be home more with her sons. She continued to help them with their homework, but was much more present with them, as she was able to act as more of a resource than as their primary teacher. They began to thrive in school.

She eventually graduated with her degree and was immediately recruited for several high-level positions with hotel restaurants. She took one of them and began to succeed immediately, rising up in the management hierarchy. However, as she kept succeeding as a mother and in her career, she found herself constantly looking for the limitations in her life, now valuing them as a guide for keeping her from the old pattern of over functioning, rather than seeing them as problems to be overcome. This idea about seeking limitation simplified her decision-making and made her much more effective in the tasks she took on. To her utter surprise, she found she was more in control of her life as she worked to do less.

Paul

Paul was a mechanic, smart but uneducated. He finished three years of high school but never graduated. He went to work for a large manufacturing company and quickly demonstrated his abilities. They recognized his talent and continued to give him raises, but he always resisted taking any promotions that made him a boss. He was very well respected by his peers and trained many new and younger employees.

He had worked at the company for 15 years when his wife went back to work after their oldest daughter graduated from high school. He became depressed, not able to identify quite what the problem was, just that he was very unhappy and not sure about the point of living. At the same time, his boss was pressing him to accept a promotion to become a foreman and to do some training for other employees at a different plant. He resisted this offer, saying he was not really capable of a position at that level.

He came to therapy for his depression, and the therapist challenged his refusal to take the promotion. The therapist did not present this as a supportive effort in recognition of his true abilities, but as a challenge to him to tolerate the anxiety of allowing himself to be competent. The therapist told him he did not have a low self-concept but a distorted one that protected him from his fear of having to be a good mechanic.

While confusing, at the same time it made sense to him. He began to experiment, first by simply refraining from making derogatory comments about himself at work, and then by gradually accepting praise from his fellow workers and boss, instead of his usual dismissal of compliments. This made him anxious, but also calm in a strange way. After significant work in therapy, he decided to accept a small promotion, which made him very anxious. Surprising himself, he was able to perform well in his new job, though he still had trouble at times when people would praise him.

The depression went away. However, he kept in contact with his therapist periodically, especially as he learned that he needed help, not because he was falling into depression, but because he was facing another situation of having to make a choice about taking on more responsibilities at work or at home. He now realized that what he needed to do for the rest of his life was to accept the anxiety of how good he was, and how powerful the pull was for him to sabotage himself by functioning below the level of his true abilities.

When considering their relationship to the world, Mary and Paul exemplify two different, but equivalent, ways people operate. For most of their lives people get along on a daily basis making decisions based on an assumption that either magnifies or minifies the possibility of a favorable outcome for their efforts. Their actions can be traced to their decisions based on assumptions of magnification or minification of what is possible. Mary is a Magnifier and Paul is a Minifier.

Decisions make you who you are

We are constantly making decisions: from the small ones, like crossing the street here instead of there, having another helping of food, or saying thank you as someone holds the door, to larger ones like buying a new coat, fixing the roof on your house, or getting extra help for your child in school. However, decisions are not made in a vacuum. People understand their own decisions, and people around them understand their decisions as making sense in some way.

The decisions make sense because they reflect a pattern. One person may be generally polite and often say thank you; someone else may be always working to maintain his house; and someone else may frequently work with a daughter to improve her grades. If any of these people made decisions different from the pattern, it would be noticeable, both to that person and to others.

My contention is that this consistency, of a current decision with patterns of previous decisions over time, serves an important function. It maintains stability, not just any stability, but the stability of the Self.

So I would argue that you are the pattern of your decisions. That means that your Self is not defined by a big decision here or there. It is defined by a pattern of decisions over time. This stability of Self, then, comes from a dynamic process, not a static one. One decision leads to another. They begin to fit together and become coordinated in such a way that a person can easily recognize themself. One remembers who they are by this stable pattern from the past, and can also project this Self into the future based on the predictability of the pattern.

This is very different from the typical assumption that the decisions a person makes depend on the situation and are independent of one another. A person considers a variety of options, decides on one, and then acts on that decision. In my framework the pattern determines the decision and the situation is secondary. The situation provides the context for making the same kind of decision over and over. From this point of view, the decision is predictable because of the pattern evident from past decisions. This is stability.

However, stability is not necessarily a good thing. Decisions to drink large amounts of alcohol every day maintain that person as an alcoholic and "stabilize" his role in his family around many problematic, but constant, interactions with his wife, his boss, and the police. The decisions each day to drink are part of a lifelong pattern of alcoholism and make sense to everyone.

Conversely, decisions can also stabilize patterns at higher levels of functioning. A teacher who continually chooses to read the newest books and go to workshops to provide her students with the most current information in the field maintains the Self of a good teacher. She keeps on reading and going to workshops, which everyone understands as her being herself.

The next step is to integrate this idea of decision-making into the Magnification/Minification framework described in the Introduction. To begin with, one could say that people make decisions from either the Magnification side of the continuum or the Minification side. A person who operates from the Mag side will generally make decisions, both big and little, that minimize the possibility of being limited. They will decide to buy the latest cell phone in order not to be left behind and miss out on having all the newest features. On the other side, the person from the Min side will choose to minimize the possibility of having too much potential. They will not want the latest clothing fad because they do not want to stand out in public.

The framework of Magnification/Minification provides an easy way to identify the patterns of decision-making for a person. It helps people understand how their pattern of making decisions from either side of the continuum stabilizes the Self. In addition, because the framework is a continuum, and not just an either/or categorization, it offers a very effective way to scale the different levels of functioning of the patterns of decision-making. This is because patterns of making decisions from the extreme ends of the continuum, from either the Magnification side or the Minification side, are less functional than patterns of decision-making closer to the Middle. Why?

Levels of functioning —

The extremes and the Middle

Decisions made from the extreme of either end are less functional because they do not offer as many options for managing the Self as those from the Middle. This requires some explanation.

As stated in the Introduction, this framework of Magnification/Minification is about managing a deep anxiety about living in the world. What does that mean? The anxiety is about surviving. In this civilized world it is not the anxiety about being attacked by an animal predator, but for some people it is about physical survival, for example, in the face of a family history of cancer or heart disease. While the anxiety is not always about physical survival, for everyone on a daily basis this anxiety is about the survival of the Self.

Most of the time people are not aware of this anxiety, because the stability of the Self is not challenged. They are protected from this anxiety by their sense of themselves. Often it is only when that sense of Self is challenged that a person experiences this anxiety, which then confirms the notion that up until then the protection was in place and working well.

Getting divorced; becoming sober; being fired from a job; leaving home; becoming a parent; having a parent die; receiving a terminal diagnosis; receiving a large inheritance; and retirement are a few examples of life events that can seriously challenge the stability of the Self. The anxiety that emerges in dealing with such events reveals the protection that was in place before that point.

That protection is the stability of the Self, which, I contend, comes from continually making decisions that define who a person is, and further, that Magnification/Minification is an effective way to understand how that person's protection works. It is important to explain more about this anxiety because it is fundamental to understanding what drives the Mag/Min dynamic.

Magnifiers make decisions based on a fear of limitations. The farther out on the continuum the Home position is from the Middle, the greater is that fear and the greater the need for protection from it. Operating from the Mag side protects the person from the fear of limitation by denying it. The denial of limitation is protective. It is the same for Minifiers. They are afraid of potential, with the fear being greater the farther the Home position is away from the Middle on the continuum. Operating from the Min side protects them from the fear of potential by denial of potential. Again: Magnifiers deny limitation and Minifiers deny potential.

However, this anxiety goes much deeper than just a fear of failure or a fear of success. Ernest Becker defined it as a life-and-death anxiety. He argued that humans are always alert to concerns about survival, but usually it does not rise to the surface of awareness, because we are protected by this very process of denial.

But why do we need denial? Becker contended that it is because of our anxiety about life as well as death. His contribution is a major one with his seminal book *Denial of Death*, and while his argument is thorough and complex, it can be distilled down to the following idea. He asserts that there is a profound paradox for the human in living in the world. On the one hand, we are a symbolic species who can use language to imagine anything we want to, including the notion that we are entirely unique, that there is no other person who is us, even that we will live forever and never die. On the other hand, we know that we have a body that is like everyone else's and that it will die. So we are very common and not unique. So which is it? Becker calls the fact that both propositions are true and that they contradict each other, the "existential paradox." He further argues that this irreconcilability is terrifying. To be aware of the fact that we can die at any moment at the very same time that we engage fully in living life—to be fully aware of both simultaneously—creates too much anxiety to handle. So most of the time, we are not aware of this conundrum. But that is exactly Becker's point: denial protects us by blocking that awareness. We need denial in order to stay sane and function in the world. He describes it this way (Becker, 1973):

> We might call this existential paradox the condition of *individuality within finitude*. Man has a symbolic identity that brings him sharply out of nature. He is a symbolic self, a creature with a name, a life history. He is a creator with a mind that soars out to speculate about atoms and infinity, who can place himself imaginatively at a point in space and contemplate bemusedly his own planet. This immense expansion, this dexterity, this ethereality, this self-consciousness gives to man literally the status of a small god in nature, as Renaissance thinkers knew.
>
> Yet, at the same time, as the Eastern sages also knew, man is a worm and food for worms. This is the paradox: he is out of

nature and hopelessly in it; he is dual, up in the stars and yet housed in a heart-pumping, breath-gasping body that once belonged to a fish and still carries the gill-marks to prove it. . . . Man is literally split in two: he has an awareness of his own splendid uniqueness in that he sticks out of nature with a towering majesty, and yet he goes back into the ground a few feet in order blindly and dumbly to rot and disappear forever. It is a terrifying dilemma to be in and to have to live with. (p. 26, emphasis in original)

This argument of Becker's is the foundation for my Mag/Min continuum. In every decision there is the possibility that it will work out (life) or that it will not (death). Both remain possibilities all the time, with every decision. As we assess each situation in order to decide what to do, we calculate the probability of a favorable or unfavorable outcome. While there are many rational factors that can go into that calculation, even with the best assessment there is always the possibility that the decision is wrong and will lead to an unfavorable outcome. To constantly allow this possibility of it being a bad decision creates too much anxiety, and so we simplify the process with an emotional calculation. As we begin to assess the situation, we assume right off (the reflex) that what we decide generally works out and any difficulties can be overcome—magnification. Or we assume right off (the reflex) that what we decide generally does not work out easily or at all—minification.

In both cases we avoid the vulnerability of having to make a decision that may not work out despite our best assessment. The Magnifier could be wrong by making a mistake of not allowing limitations, and the Minifier could be wrong by making the mistake of not allowing potential. That risk of failure can be very high in a particular situation, such as deciding to have surgery. Or it can be high in a long term pattern of many decisions, like drinking too much and ignoring the consequences, or dismissing opportunities for promotions thereby sabotaging one's career. So we protect ourselves from that risk by an emotional calculation that distorts the risk. The Magnifier minimizes the risk and the Minifier maximizes the risk.

The closer the person's Home position is to the Middle of the continuum, the less distortion of the risk. It is important to clarify here that less distortion of the risk allows a better assessment of the outcome as favorable or unfavorable, but it *does not ensure* a favorable outcome. If it would be a bad decision to do something, a good assessment would indicate that, and both the Mag and the Min, operating from a position closer to the Middle from either side, would come to that same conclusion. Of course, the same is true for both Mag and Min when each assesses the outcome as favorable from positions closer to the Middle.

The two sides of Magnification and Minification represent patterns of decision-making then, that are positions of denial that block the awareness of the existential paradox, and these patterns come to define the Self, who we are.

It should be noted that there is no exact Middle point, because that would represent the terror which Becker posits. Realistically, there always has to be some denial, but closer to the Middle there is less. On the continuum this deeper, existential anxiety about survival does emerge more the closer one moves toward the Middle, because there is less rejection of the opposite end. Toward the Middle, Magnifiers allow more limitation (but never cross to the other side), and Minifiers allow more potential (similarly never crossing to the other side). This means that Mags who make decisions on the basis of accepting more limitations have to live with some anxiety about not having gone all the way, having missed an important opportunity, or having let other people down. For Mins, it means making decisions on the basis of accepting more potential, and having to live with some anxiety about having gone too far, having acted without considering all the alternatives, or having deceived people into letting them take charge.

Becker framed his idea in the existential terms of life and death, which is the deepest anxiety. What I have done with my framework of Mag/Min is to extend this dynamic of denial into all the decisions we make in the course of life, both the most difficult ones that significantly impact our lives and the trivial ones of daily life. This extension of a very powerful dynamic is what makes the framework so practical and useful in changing the Self, because there is constant access to the possibility of change through all the decisions we make all the time.

The point of writing this book is to present the possibility of changing the Self to function better in the world. On the continuum this means changing one's patterns of decision-making to move the Home position closer to the Middle. In terms of existential anxiety and denial, this means that there is less denial, less protection, the more one moves toward the Middle. While this does cost that protection, the payoff is more calmness and higher functioning, because there is more openness and flexibility to engage in life with all the ups and downs, with less effort going into trying to control the anxiety.

Based on this fundamental idea about anxiety that underlies my Mag/Min framework, I will refer to the Mag/Min framework throughout the rest of the book as a mechanism of denial. I will call each side of Magnification and Minification a "denial mode." I will call the Magnifier's efforts to allow more limitation, thereby increasing the ability to function more effectively, "moving toward the Middle." In the same way, I will call the Minifier's efforts to allow more potential, thereby increasing the ability to function more effectively, "moving toward the Middle." The following chart displays the basic continuum, identifying characteristics of the Middle and of the extremes at either end, which will then be explained.

Behavioral Characteristics

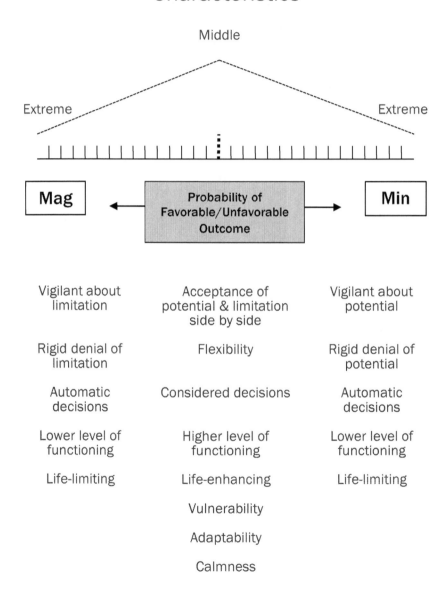

Figure 1.1

Notice how the behaviors at the extremes of both Magnification and Minification are described in the same way, with the only difference between them being the anxiety about the opposite. Also, note the contrast in how the Middle is described as the more moderate position that is higher functioning, and which is characterized by vulnerability and calmness. You will also see a dashed line angled up from each side toward the Middle. This represents the fact that there is a natural pull toward the extremes as people manage the anxiety described above. It requires work to move "up" toward the Middle. All of these characteristics identified in this chart will be apparent in the explanation below of the dynamics of the Middle, and the different levels of functioning defined by operating from farther out on either side. They will also be part of the development of the framework in later chapters and subsequent charts.

From the Mag side of the continuum, the person has a Self, defined by always making decisions that counter threats of limitations, based on the fear that they are not able to overcome every obstacle and deal with that vulnerability continually. Doing that defines who they are. From the Min side, the person has a Self, defined by always making decisions that counter threats of potential, based on the fear that they would be powerful and have to deal with the vulnerability of having to continually be strong. For each of them, this pattern defines who they are.

This pattern of operating from either side, Magnification or Minification, functions in this way to protect people from the anxiety about survival by providing a stable Self. However, as stated above, that stability can vary in how functional it is in how one lives life. This variability comes from how much that protective mechanism of Magnification or Minification can adapt to changing circumstances. The more rigid it is, the more automatic the response to every situation, regardless of what kind of threat or challenge is presented.

The Magnifier, who is always on guard for any suggestion of limitation, and always works to figure out how to meet the challenge and not ever lose or walk away, will miss out on opportunities to have less stress and less wasted energy, money, or time by trying too hard. There will be some times where accepting limitation is the best option, but a person operating from the extreme end of the Mag continuum is limited in their ability to adapt to that situation.

Similarly, the Minifier, who is always on guard for any hint of potential, and always works to figure out how to avoid the challenge and not ever take it on or succeed, will miss out on opportunities to have less stress and less wasted energy, money, or time by avoiding potential at all costs. There will be some times where accepting potential is the best option, but a person operating from the extreme end of the Min continuum is limited in their ability to adapt to that situation.

In this way, the people operating more from the Middle on the continuum are calmer. They are able to trust themselves more in being able to handle situations as they come up, more than people farther out on the continuum, who are more anxious because they have to be ready to prevent problems. They have to be vigilant about limitations that could be harmful, or potential that could require being strong, all before knowing what is really necessary to cope. In the Middle people are calmer, but also more vulnerable, as they take their chances dealing with challenges as they come up. The calmness comes from trusting that the Self will be able to handle the challenge, and deal with the outcome whether it is successful or not. This calmness, and the vulnerability that comes with it, allow people to make better decisions about the challenge because their response is not automatic, driven by the need to protect the Self.

So the higher level of functioning is more toward the Middle on the continuum. This is where there are more options for the person as they make decisions in response to challenges that come up both daily and at significant points in one's life, because there is less distortion of the probability of a favorable outcome.

An important factor in the ability to allow a more considered response to the Mag/Min reflex in decision-making is the ability to distinguish between feeling and thinking. Here anxiety, presented in the section in the Introduction about why the work is so hard, is critical. The ability to distinguish feeling and thinking is reflected in the person's ability to tolerate anxiety. To make decisions based on feelings decreases the odds of making good decisions over time. Impulsive decisions may be good ones, but only occasionally, depending on luck and favorable circumstances, because they are responses to anxiety. In that way they limit choices, because there is no larger perspective of thinking to recognize patterns (for example, always trying to meet one's own needs first, or always trying to please others), and be able to make decisions that have a better probability of positive outcomes in the long run.

In addition, decisions based on feelings are more likely to be responses to the anxiety, not just in that one person, but in the larger system of one's family, for example. Then those decisions of the individual actually become part of the patterns of the whole system's ways of managing the anxiety (for example, with a violent and extroverted family, or a reclusive and introverted family).

Higher functioning equals the ability to sort through feelings by what is primarily an emotional response and what makes sense upon reflection. In this way, a person can recognize patterns and then make decisions based on this larger perspective. Then the person has more options, because they are not as limited by the automatic response that maintains the patterns, both of the individual person and as part of the larger system. And, with more choices comes higher functioning, because one has a wider range of options to respond more effectively to varying challenges that come up.

It should be noted here that making decisions based on intuition is not the same as making them impulsively on feelings. The difference is that the process of intuition is based on reflection, because there is an awareness of a perspective. While it is not a perspective derived from thoughts, it is one that comes from a sense of the situation and a consideration of the factors involved in the possible outcomes.

The Magnifier who operates closer to the Middle, not as far out toward the extreme of the continuum, has the ability to allow some limitation. This is a strength (contrary to what these people usually feel), because it gives them the option to make a better decision based on a calmer assessment of the situation, rather than yielding only to an automatic response based on the attempt to avoid anxiety.

Minifiers who operate closer to the Middle, not as far out toward the extreme of the continuum, have the ability to allow some potential. This is also a strength (contrary to their assumption that they don't have any), because it gives them the option to make a better decision based on a calmer assessment of the situation, rather than yielding only to an automatic response based on the attempt to avoid anxiety.

These different points on the continuum, from the extreme ends to the Middle, make a difference, because they determine how one lives one's life. It is not just a matter of whether one makes a good or a bad decision, because it is the patterns of decisions one makes over time that impact how one copes with the inevitable challenges of life. Automatic decisions based in operating from farther out on the extremes of the continuum, from either Magnification or Minification, are more distorted and restrict one's ability to live life to the fullest. Full participation in life requires that one be able to both accept the pain of the downs and the excitement of the ups. People farther out toward either end of the continuum, Mag or Min, can do one or the other very well, but do poorly in allowing both. The stability of the Self, operating more from the Middle comes from an acceptance of both, trusting in the ability to make good decisions depending on the situation, whether acceptance of loss is the most adaptive response or allowing the excitement is the most adaptive. The response cannot be predetermined by the pattern of always operating from Magnification or Minification, but must be assessed continually as situations come up.

Operating more from the Middle enables the person to develop more adaptive responses over time because they have the flexibility to choose alternative options that don't come up in their usual decision-making process, and build a larger repertoire of possible responses to use in different situations. Then they can trust their ability to call upon this repertoire to handle unfamiliar challenges in the future.

With this increased capacity to handle the unfamiliar, one can live life more fully by taking more risks (more limitation for Mags and more potential for Mins), because a person can trust their ability to make better decisions based on more realistic assessments of the probability of a favorable outcome.

Of course, what comes along with allowing risks, though based on sounder decision-making and higher functioning, is the unknown, the feeling of vulnerability that emerges because one is deviating from the stability of the pattern of the automatic decision, and will have to face situations as they come up and decide what to do. With the higher level of functioning in the Middle, this vulnerability is actually calming, as the person is not so consumed by anxiety about success or failure, but is more grounded in trusting Self.

Change of points on the continuum

Now what about these different levels of functioning, these different points on the continuum? Can they change? If so, can they change just a little, or a lot?

This book is all about change. I assume that it is indeed possible to change one's Home position on the continuum. The Home position identifies the extent to which the Self is stabilized by patterns of decision-making that are more or less extreme. This book presents a way to move the Home position closer to the Middle from wherever it is on the continuum. That way is to change the Self by changing the patterns of decision-making.

Before proceeding to describe the change process, it is important to remind the reader, as stated at the beginning of this chapter, that the stability of the Self is maintained by the patterns of decisions that a person makes over time, and to emphasize that those patterns reflect a dynamic process, not a static or linear one, of continual decisions made and actions taken. The stability comes from the ongoing process that one could think of as constantly in motion, looping between decisions and actions.

Decisions do not come out of nowhere. All decisions are part of a pattern. They flow out of previous ones and are part of maintaining that person's Self. A person decides to go out for a walk. She has already had the idea to do this and then gets up and goes out the door and begins to walk. She takes a walk every once in a while, so this is not unusual for her to do. The idea is not brand new to her and it is not an effort to get up and do it. As she is walking, she meets some neighbors who say hello and are not surprised to see her. They know her as a person who walks periodically. She realizes the air is fresh and she is glad she decided to walk today. The action of walking loops back and reinforces the decision she made. Tomorrow she may decide to walk again, remembering how much she enjoyed the one today.

As this example demonstrates, decisions, and the actions that follow, cannot be separated, as they continually interact, each influencing the other, but creating an overall pattern that can be very stable.

So then, what does it take to change the pattern? Does one interrupt the pattern through the behavior or through the decisions? This book presents a framework in which a person changes the pattern first by experimenting with different behaviors (different from the pattern) as the person becomes aware of the pattern of behaviors and recognizes the decision points that lead to those behaviors. The ability to recognize these decision points varies, basically by how far away from the Middle the Home position is, because the decisions will be more "automatic" at the extremes, where they are more determined by magnification or minification, with less awareness of options as the decisions are being made.

Again, notice that it takes effort to move the Home position "up" toward the Middle to counter the pull toward the more automatic decision-making toward the ends of the continuum. Nonetheless, my assumption is that any movement closer to the Middle, regardless of how far out the Home position is on the continuum or how large the movement is, results in some degree of higher functioning, because it allows a wider range of options when the person is challenged. See Figure 1.2, which depicts this with the inclusion of the directions of change from either side.

Behavioral Characteristics

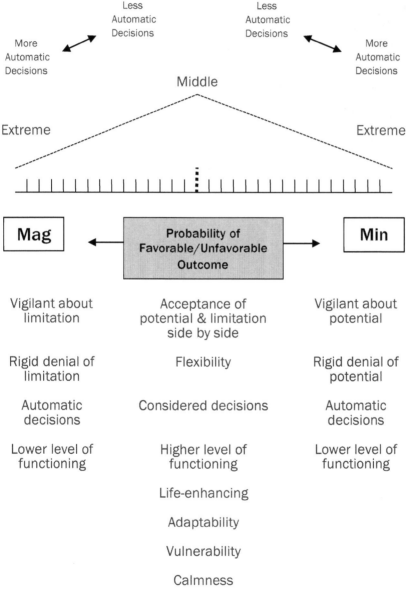

Figure 1.2

There are two caveats about this question of change. One is to remember that the only change possible is from the Home position, in either direction, toward the Middle (which is improved functioning) or toward the end of the continuum (which is regressed functioning), never across the Middle (See Figure 1.2). This important axiom was introduced in the Introduction and the rationale for it will be presented in the following chapters.

The other caveat is that a person's expectation about change will be very different depending precisely on which side of the continuum one operates from. This framework itself actually challenges the stability of the Self, simply as people begin to understand it. It is that powerful. People from the Mag side will overestimate the amount of change that is possible, seeing this framework as a powerful tool to achieve even more, and people from the Min side will underestimate the amount of change possible, seeing this framework as confirmation of how little is really possible.

In addition, it makes no sense to try to define specific points on the continuum indicating particular assumptions or behaviors, because the framework is not developed or tested enough to sustain efforts to define particular points on a scale. The usefulness of the continuum is to provide a way to identify a *direction*. People on the Mag side are going in the wrong direction if they see this framework as a way to control their anxiety about limitation. People on the Min side are going in the wrong direction if they see this framework as a way to be even more careful about not taking risks. *The question is always: which way is the Middle?*

However, the continuum can be useful as one compares one's patterns of decision-making from one point in time to another in order to assess whether one has made changes in moving the Home position toward the Middle or not, and in a crude way whether it is a little or a lot. I resist any attempts to define these points more specifically, because of my assumption that no one operates from the Middle, which is the only position from which a person could define what the points are on the other side from which they operate.

So given the possibility of change and the understanding of the use of the continuum, it is now time to take the next step in identifying your Home position.

Chapter 2

The Home Position

Identifying the Home position

The Home position identifies the basic pattern of operation for people as they act on most of their decisions. It is a position driven by a basic assumption of either Magnification or Minification in the face of challenge.

Chapter 1 presented the foundation for this conceptualization of Magnification and Minification, and described the general patterns from either side. This chapter will present these patterns in terms of specific behaviors, so the reader can identify their own Home position and begin to recognize the patterns in others.

Some people know immediately where their Home position is. They recognize that their basic assumption is one of either Magnification or Minification. Very often this first impression turns out to be accurate. Other people are initially confused, but then can identify it accurately after a while, but others still struggle, as they sometimes think it is one and then think it is the other. It is very important to be able to correctly identify whether the Home position is Mag or Min. I will explain this more thoroughly later, but for now let me say the reason for getting it right is that then one knows which way the Middle is. For example, a person may incorrectly assume they operate from the Min side, when they really operate from the Mag side, always trying to achieve more, thinking it is necessary for success. As a result, they continually try harder, afraid to ever let down and not strive for the best, which is actually moving farther out to the extreme of Magnification on the continuum. Similarly, a person incorrectly assuming they are a Magnifier may try continually to restrict their efforts to take chances and be expansive, which is actually moving farther out to the extreme of Minification on the continuum.

As described in Chapter 1, one of the fundamental assumptions of this framework, which has been validated over and over again in my experience with people, is that everyone operates from a Home position of either Magnification or Minification, one or the other, never both, and never sometimes one and sometimes the other. A person does not go back and forth from one side of the continuum to the other. Nor does a person operate from the Magnification side in some situations and from the Minification side in others.

Chart of behaviors

As I present the chart of behaviors now, to help the reader identify their Home position, it is very important that you focus the effort on simply identifying which side your Home position is on, not at what point it falls on the scale. It is eventually very useful to assess how far out the Home position is from the Middle, but it is essential to first establish which side the Home position is on. Otherwise, the initial reactivity generated simply by the anxiety of identifying one side or the other will distort an accurate assessment of the distance of the Home position from the Middle. This is because people will try to find the point on the scale where they fall, precisely as a function of which side their Home position is on. Magnifiers will try to assess themselves and believe that they are not extreme, and most likely will identify a point too close to the Middle because they fear the limitation of being an extreme Mag. Similarly, Minifiers will skew their assessment to be too far away from the Middle, fearing to identify their Home position accurately as less limited.

This "scale" is intended only to provide a crude sense of a general point of distance from the Middle. Beginning with the next chapter on change, I will use the continuum to plot gross, but clear, changes in patterns of decision-making. Figure 2.1 offers one way, a list of behaviors, to help people identify a Home position on one side or the other of the continuum.

Decision-making Behaviors

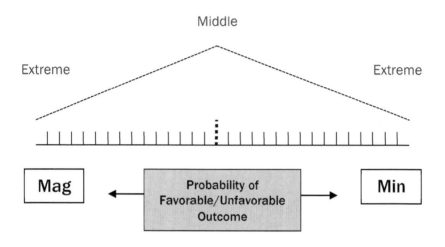

Middle

Extreme   Extreme

| Mag | Probability of Favorable/Unfavorable Outcome | Min |

Handles anxiety about limitation by minimizing risk	Handles anxiety about potential by maximizing risk
Asserts failure is unacceptable	Assumes failure is inevitable
When challenged, acts to overcome obstacles	When challenged, acts to avoid obstacles
Acts to maximize gains	Acts to minimize losses
Embraces risk	Plays it safe
Functions above basic abilities	Functions below basic abilities
Primitive response - Fight	Primitive response - Flight

Figure 2.1

Which are you most afraid of?

One of the litmus tests I have come to use with people when they cannot tell which side of the continuum they operate from, is to ask them what they are most afraid of: magnifying or minifying. Min people will say they are afraid of potential, like too much success for example, or of dominating others, or of being conceited. They are never afraid of limitation. They can accept that easily. Mags will talk about being afraid of any limitation, like having to acknowledge not being strong enough, or not able to succeed in a task, or having made a mistake. They are never afraid of being too powerful or of being right.

A related test is to ask how people would respond when seriously challenged, for example with a life-threatening medical diagnosis. Before this they may never have been challenged enough to recognize what their deeper assumptions are. The behaviors, and the assumptions behind them, reflect the denial mode of Magnification or Minification.

Over the years I have gathered some typical denial modes from students in my classes who have had to write a "Becker paper" presenting their denial mode. Their assignment is to present the basic assumption of their denial mode, the behavior that manifests it, and how that denial mode protects them. It is very challenging because they have to explore the assumptions that protect them from the anxiety about the other side. Many times I have heard how it is the most difficult paper they have ever had to write, and then afterward how it has been the most rewarding. Below is a list of a few representative examples of people, both Magnifiers and Minifiers, which can help readers find their Home position by recognizing similar patterns of assumptions and behaviors in their own lives.

Examples of denial modes

"I am a special person, and I need to be very selective about who I date." This is a behavior of continually sabotaging relationships that are actually developing and growing. This is the Magnifier mode, grounded in the fear of being limited by someone else, by a commitment to a relationship.

"I am basically content in my current relationship." The behavior here is to continually make excuses for the partner, knowing it is actually an unsatisfying relationship. This is the Minifier mode, grounded in the fear of taking the initiative to end the relationship, and move on to a better one.

"I don't need anyone's help because I can do it better myself." The behavior is to always take on all tasks in all areas, including the roles of wife and mother. This is the Magnifier mode, grounded in the fear of discovering one's own weaknesses or inadequacies, and of needing others.

"I like to take my time making decisions." The behavior is to procrastinate and never really take the next step to move on to the next life stage. This is the Minifier mode, grounded in the fear of making a major decision that indeed changes one's life.

Even accepting the axiom that the Home position is on one side or the other, people often cannot clearly identify their own Home position, not to mention being unable to identify whether another person is a Magnifier or Minifier. There are two major sources for this confusion. I will clarify each of them in the next two sections by introducing two additional concepts, which will serve to explain the framework in more depth and should resolve the confusion.

Primary and secondary denial modes —

Mag and Min

People often get confused because it seems a person goes back and forth on the continuum, sometimes a Magnifier and sometimes a Minifier. To resolve this dilemma, it is important to include an additional concept, which comes directly from Bowen theory. It is the concept of the Social self.

Some years ago, in presenting this material to my class, I used myself as an example, identifying my Home position as that of Magnification. My assumption was that I had a good self-concept, saw myself as a good father, a good teacher, a therapist with a very successful practice, highly respected by most people. Then one time it did not work.

As I talked with the class about using the test of which you fear more, too much potential or too much limitation, I realized I was more afraid of potential. I am very comfortable with limitation. That contradicted my whole presentation and was very upsetting to me. To present material that does not make sense to you as the teacher in a classroom is not a good situation. When, as a teacher or as a therapist, some of my ideas don't work or seem unclear, I take them back to myself and apply the ideas to my own life. When my students keep struggling to understand one of my assignments, I may try to write that paper myself. When clients sometimes question my suggestions, I reflect on whether this idea is more pertinent in my life than theirs, and figure out what part, if any, applies to them. So I went home and experimented with the idea that I might operate from the Minification side. Immediately everything fell into place as I looked at my basic assumptions and how I had lived my life. It was a great relief to get it right, but now I needed to figure out why I had made that mistake.

As presented earlier in this chapter, some people can identify their Home position immediately. My assumption about them is that they have easy access to anxiety about being challenged, either because they have been significantly challenged already in their lives, or because their family or other systems function with their operating from this position of a straightforward denial mode. On the other hand, people who are confused may well have a denial mode like mine that is not straightforward. This all has to do with the Basic and Social self.

In my framework the Social self is a secondary mode of denial. Bowen called it the "pseudo self" and distinguished it from the "basic self." He explained it this way (1978):

> The basic self is a definite quality illustrated by such "I position" stances as: "These are my beliefs and convictions. This is what I am, and who I am, and what I will do, or not do." The basic self may be changed from *within* self on the basis of new knowledge and experience. The basic self *is not negotiable in the relationship system* in that it is not changed by coercion or pressure, or to gain approval, or enhance one's standing with others. There is another fluid, shifting level of self, which I call the "pseudo-self," which makes it difficult to assign fixed values to the basic self, and which is best understood with functional concepts. The pseudo-self is made up of a mass of heterogeneous facts, beliefs, and principles acquired through the relationship system in the prevailing emotion. These include facts learned because one is supposed to know them, and beliefs borrowed from others or accepted in order to enhance one's position in relationship to others. *The pseudo-self, acquired under the influence of the relationship system, is negotiable in the relationship system.* The pseudo-self can accept a plausible-sounding philosophy under the emotional influence of the moment, or it can just as easily adopt an opposite philosophy to oppose the relationship system. (p. 473, emphasis in original)

Bowen calls what I identify as the Social self, "pseudo," implying that it is not real. I have learned that the Social self is a very important component of the whole Self, because of our social nature as humans. My assumption is that there is no such thing as a Self that exists independently of the selves of other people. My contention in this framework is that there are two dimensions of the Self, Basic and Social, and that the Basic self is primary and the Social is secondary. However, I maintain that there is an essential coordination between them, and that the Self overall emerges from this ongoing coordination. I would characterize the difference between the Basic self and the Social self in the following way. Basic self: "I know who I am as I reflect about myself." Social self: "I know who I am as I interact with others and reflect about myself in that interaction."

In terms of Mag/Min, a person can be a Magnifier with the Home position marking the Basic self on that side of the continuum, and have a Social self that is the same (magnifier) or different (minifier). Similarly a person can be a Minifier with a Social self that is mag or min. The Home position defines the Basic self and that is the Self that is the locus of change for the work to be done using this Mag/Min framework. However the Social self is intricately connected to that Basic self in a sophisticated coordination whether the Social is mag or min.

So the reader can be clear, when I refer to the "Self" I mean the whole self, composed of the coordination of the Basic and Social dimensions. In the text this whole self will be capitalized ("Self"). The two dimensions of this self will be in lower case, but with the identified dimensions capitalized as Basic or Social ("Basic self" and "Social self"). When referring to a person's configuration of Basic and Social self together, I will place the Basic first, followed by a slash and then the Social. Also, I will display the Basic in upper case and the Social in lower case. Thus the four configurations are: MAG/mag; MAG/min; MIN/min; and MIN/mag. (A more thorough explanation of the dynamics of the Self and its foundation in the processes of language will be presented in Chapter 5, "The Self as Narrative.")

The Basic self is, as Bowen says, characterized by the stances of fundamental beliefs and convictions and what a person knows about who they are and what they will and will not do. However, Bowen implies that the "pseudo" or Social self is more fluid and malleable, as it is "negotiable." While I agree that the Basic self is the foundational self that does not fluctuate in relationships with others, I see the Social self as much more constant in its coordination with the Basic self. Given that the Social is the part of the Self that emerges out of the interactions with others, how that happens can vary widely depending on the different relationships, but *the coordination remains constant*. For example if a Magnifier has a Social self that is the same, also mag, that Self will not change to a Social min, just as a Magnifier with a Social min will not change to a mag in social interactions. Likewise, if a Minifier has a Social self that is the same, also min, that Self will not change to a Social mag, just as a Minifier with a Social mag will not change to a min in social interactions

How this coordination works depends on the assumptions of the person's Basic self and how the Social self functions to maintain that Home position as Mag or Min. (The dynamics of coordination between the Basic and Social selves will be explained more thoroughly in the next chapter on change.) What is essential is to first identify the Home position of the Basic self and then determine whether the Social is the same or different.

For some people, their Social self is based in an assumption of Minification and so is their Basic self, just as for some Magnifiers the Social self is the same as the Basic self. It is straightforward and clear. For others like myself, their Basic self is based in an assumption of Minification, but if not seriously challenged, it looks and functions more like a person from the Magnification side. The person acts *as if* the probability of a favorable outcome is high (like a Magnifier). Similarly, for a Magnifier with an opposite Social self as a min, the person acts *as if* the probability of a favorable outcome is low (like a

Minifier). So for these people the identification of the Home position is not straightforward and not as clear because the basic and social modes are not the same.

The question sometimes comes up about whether the denial modes being the same or opposite indicates differences in levels of functioning. My current thinking is that this difference in denial modes is a manifestation of patterns that have probably developed over time, beginning with one's family, and become part of the dynamics of balancing those family systems and other social systems for that person. For some people it is the same denial mode that functions to stabilize the balance in their family, and for others the opposite denial mode is stabilizing. How these patterns of same and opposite develop and function is an aspect of the framework that needs to be explored further in the future to understand the process.

This dual denial mode for both Magnification and Minification does add another layer of sorting to the identification process, but it does not at all change the identification of the Home position as the position of the Basic self, identified by the assumption behind the response to the reflex triggered by having one's Self seriously challenged. Rather than adding to the confusion of identifying one's Home position, this additional layer of a secondary denial mode can actually help people get to their basic assumption on the continuum as either Magnification or Minification, as they can distinguish the Basic and Social.

Here is another chart (Figure 2.2) to help clarify graphically this additional component or layer.

Basic and Social Selves

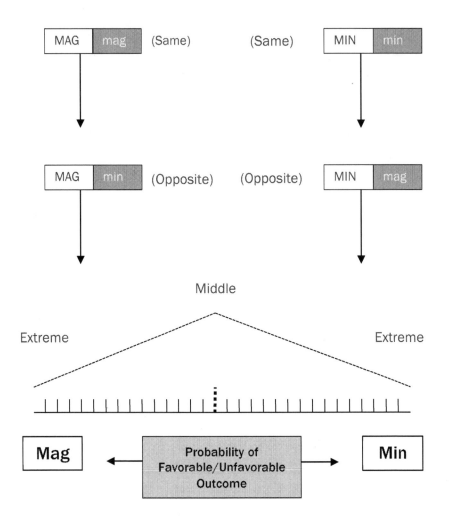

Figure 2.2

This chart simply depicts the two profiles of the primary or Basic denial mode on the Magnification side and on the Minification side. The top row is the profile of the Basic and Social being the same, Mag/mag and Min/min. The bottom row shows the profile of Basic and Social being opposite, Mag/min and Min/mag. Note that the arrows come from the Basic box because that is what determines the Home position. If one's denial mode is seriously challenged, the Basic level will determine the functioning

Another distinction about the two configurations of the Basic and Social as the same versus opposite concerns the reactions of others. When the two selves are the same, people generally expect the MAG/mag to operate socially as a Magnifier. In the same way people expect the MIN/min to operate socially as a Minifier. However confusion can arise when others have to deal with a MAG/min or a MIN/mag. If they only know the Social self of MAG/min they get surprised if the Basic Mag comes out when the person feels threatened and no longer acts socially as if they are a Minifier. In the same way people get surprised if the MIN/mag no longer acts like a Magnifier when challenged.

When the Basic and Social are the same, there is not this kind of confusion, but there still may be some discrepancies between the Basic and Social. A MAG/mag may behave socially as "more" mag or "less" mag (but not min) than they really are as a Basic Mag. Similarly, a MIN/min may behave socially as "more" min or "less" min (but not mag) than they really are as a Basic Min. These discrepancies are a matter of degree. The observer may be unclear about how far the Home position is from the Middle, but not about which side of the continuum the person's Home position is on.

Despite all these considerations of the variables involved in the functioning of the Basic and Social self, the simple take-away for the reader is to focus first on identifying the position of the Basic self as on one side or the other of the continuum. Sorting out the Social as the same or opposite may be helpful in determining the Basic, or it may not. If it is not helpful at first, continue to focus the exploration on the Basic and let go of the effort to determine the Social. Later, when the Basic is identified, you can then consider how you act socially "as if" you are a Mag or a Min. Or you may just read on and return to this chapter and the task of determining the Social as you understand more about the framework and yourself.

Mag and Min reflex — The whole and the details

Sometimes the distinction between the Basic and Social self is still not enough to resolve the confusion about whether a person is a Magnifier or a Minifier. If one is not clear about the Basic self, it is difficult to establish the distinction of the Social self. This section builds upon the Gestalt concept of figure/ground that was presented in the Introduction, and relates directly to the dynamics of the Basic self. It takes that conceptualization of perception from Gestalt psychology, and adds the variable of a primary focus on the whole versus the details.

One can distinguish between a Mag and a Min by recognizing how a person perceives a situation in regard to the overall whole versus the specific details. For the Mag the whole is figural and fills the immediate perception, while the details remain in the background. It is the reverse for the Min, who focuses on all the details immediately, and leaves the larger whole in the background. This is a reflex; it happens automatically. However this difference in whether the whole or the details are figural can lead to much confusion in determining whether a person is Mag or Min, because of the different decisions these perceptions lead to.

Sometimes a Mag will decide to do something that has a low probability of working out. They do it anyway, but they may devote an excessive amount of time and energy attending to the details, assuming that every detail is critical for the whole task to work out. Or they may choose to do it but ignore the details, assuming it will all work out somehow.

What is confusing is that a Min can do the same thing but for the opposite reasons. They decide to do something that likewise has a low probability of working out. They too spend an enormous amount of time and energy on the details, but assume that it is important to make the attempt even though in the end it will probably not be successful. Or they may choose to do it and ignore the details, because there are just too many and it probably won't make a difference for the outcome in the end.

So both choose to say "yes" when they should say "no" because the probability of a favorable outcome is low. But observing their behavior of attending to the details or ignoring them looks the same for both the Magnifier and the Minifier. However, if you can get to the assumptions behind their behaviors, it becomes clear that while their behaviors may be the same, their assumptions about them are the opposite ones of Magnification and Minification, which will be explained below.

The same is true when both Mag and Min say "no" when they should say "yes," because the probability of a favorable outcome is high. The Magnifier declines because there are too many details to attend to, and while it would work out, it is just not worth the effort to sort through them all. The Minifier declines, again because there are too many details to attend to, but also because it is hopeless in the end to sort through them all.

All of this can certainly be confusing for an outside observer, but it is especially problematic if this is you because then you do not know which way the Middle is. This needs further explanation.

Both of the situations above of saying "yes" or "no" were presented from reactive positions on either side of the continuum. Deciding to say "yes" or "no" depending on an all-or-nothing focus on the whole or details, is a distortion of a good assessment of the probability of a favorable outcome that occurs from a position farther from the Middle.

What is missing for each of them is the ability to allow a figure/ground flow in which the background can emerge into the foreground so that the Mag can begin to see some of the details and the Min can see more of the whole. To do this would be a change to move toward the Middle of the continuum for both of them.

For the Mag this would mean allowing a greater awareness of the amount or complexity of all the details, and then assessing whether this much effort is or is not worth it. In one situation in which the actual probability of a favorable outcome is low, even though the Magnifier can see how to succeed, they are better off deciding not to do the task (limitation). In another situation when they allow more awareness of the details, and can see how some of the details but not all (limitation), are important for success, they can take on the task. But they need to limit themselves to select only a few, instead of dismissing them all with the global assumption that somehow it will all work out.

For the Min, a move toward the Middle would be to allow greater awareness of how the details contribute to the whole, and then assess whether this much effort to focus on all the minute details is worth it or not. In one situation, even though there are a lot of details, they can see that only several are important for success of the whole task and they are better off choosing to do it (potential), trusting that this is enough for the project to succeed rather than focusing on all the details. So they say "yes" to the decision. In another situation, by allowing more awareness of the whole, they can see how there are just too many details, and trying to attend to all of them is not worth the effort, trusting that they are better off saying "no" to the task.

With the Home position closer to the Middle they both end up operating from the same basis for the assessment of a favorable outcome, which is to consider the larger task and how the steps involved go together. Their immediate reflex is to focus on one or the other, not to allow a flow back and forth between them.

Here are a few examples. Two people go to the gym regularly to work out. They are both obsessive about it and go even when they have an injury. The Mag's attitude is that they have to go anyway because the injury is not that serious (it is) and they don't want to lose the level of fitness they have worked so hard to achieve. The Min's attitude is they have to go anyway because they can't afford to lose more fitness because they are at such a low level to begin with.

They both should say "no" because the probability of a favorable outcome to the workout, when they have a serious injury, is low. The Mag could do this if they could see how some of the particular exercises pose a serious risk of making the current injury worse or of introducing a new one. The Min could do this if they could see that missing a day or two is not really going to impact their overall level of fitness especially in the long term.

Two people are faced with the challenge of cleaning up their closets and sorting through all the things they have accumulated over the years. The Mag looks at all the stuff and decides not to bother because there is just too much even though there is barely room to store any more in them. The Min looks at it all and decides the same thing. It is too much. They both should say "yes" because the closets are no longer functional for them, and the situation is only going to get worse as they buy more.

The move to the Middle for the Mag is to start sorting through items, and begin to see that they can make progress on the whole project if they pick and choose what items need to be saved and what ones need to be discarded and not try to accomplish the task all at once. For the Min the move is also to attend to the details but with the recognition that small steps do indeed make a big difference ultimately in the space that becomes available with all of the closets sorted out.

As you can see from these examples as Mags and Mins make moves toward the Middle, their decision-making process begins to look similar, as they allow their awareness to flow back and forth between focusing on the specific details and the overall whole. But they get there from opposite sides of the continuum. Farther out from the Middle the awareness of both whole and detail is more limited for both. So the difference in the basis for making the decision to say "yes" or "no" is more apparent from these more extreme positions where the perception of the whole as figural for the Mag and details for the Min is more rigid.

In regard to the previous section on the Basic and Social self, it is important to remember that the explanation in this current section about the figure/ground dynamic of the whole and the details, refers to that process as it occurs in the Basic self, not the Social. It refers to this perception as it is a primitive reflex and happens immediately, not to the dynamics of the Social self that functions more as an adaptation in the social system.

As these two previous sections demonstrate, one cannot ascertain reliably whether a person is a Magnifier or a Minifier, either oneself or others, by just observing the behavior. To make the determination of the Home position as Mag or Min, one has to know the person's assumptions behind their behavior. When the behavior is confusing, it is very helpful to work to distinguish the Basic from the Social self, and to separate out whether the primary reflex is to focus on the whole or the details.

With the Home position identified, having sorted through any of these additional clarifications, the next step is to address the issue of change, moving the Home position more to the Middle.

Chapter 3

Change

Why would anyone want to change their basic denial mode of Magnification or Minification? I have discovered that the best answer to that question is: "Only if you have to." Then, the next question is: "Why choose this particular framework to make a change?" The best answer to that is: "Because it works."

There are as many reasons for why people would feel that they have to change as there are people in the various situations of their lives. In the end, it comes down to simply realizing they cannot go on with the same patterns, and are therefore willing to take a reasonable risk to change. That is the basis for my clients doing the hard work of therapy; for my students allowing themselves to experiment with thinking differently in order to learn; and for myself realizing I could no longer go on as I had been in my family life and my career.

Examples of reasons to change

- Accepting the likelihood that this third failed marriage probably indicates a problem
- Becoming aware of her need to face her serious concerns about whether to stay with her husband
- Knowing that one's temper will eventually get him into serious trouble
- Seeing that his problem of chronic job losses is not all about his employers
- Having a sense that her drinking has become more than social

- Acknowledging that living in constant debt is not just the way it is these days, but is more of a problem of one's out-of-control spending
- Beginning to think that the constant arguments with one's children is about more than just their being that way
- Recognizing that the eight-year cutoff from one's family has gone on too long and is not healthy
- Realizing she needs to deal with her unhappiness in this unfulfilling job
- Admitting to himself that he needs to get to the doctor because something has probably been wrong for quite a while

From this framework of Mag/Min, any movement toward change requires taking action that increases anxiety and vulnerability. On the charts, this direction could be characterized as movement toward the Middle from either of the two sides of the continuum. The Magnifier risks taking action that moves them toward the Middle, which is away from a more rigid denial mode of Magnification, thereby allowing more limitation. The Minifier moves toward the Middle by allowing potential and not jumping back to a more rigid position of Minification.

This next chart, Figure 3.1, is a longitudinal one that adds a third dimension to the previous ones that have displayed the continuum as a 2D diagram, with the Middle as the apex from either side. The third dimension here is time. This chart depicts the pattern of decisions a person makes over the course of their lifetime along the length of the diagram. Look again at the front cover. People picture this chart with a variety of images. Some see it as a tent; others as a piece of paper creased down the middle standing on its edges; or similarly, as a hardcover book spread open on its cover. However you visualize it, there are several elements that may be intuitive but bear some explanation.

This is *one* continuum with two ends and a middle. Mag and Min at the "edges" are extreme points that indicate greater distortion on this one continuum of two sides, not two separate dynamics of Magnification and Minification. The Middle is not a static Home position; but rather a "peak" that one moves "up" toward from either of the more extreme positions farther out on the continuum. It takes effort and work to move the stable Home position up toward the Middle on the continuum, but that new Home position can become stable as a person manages the forces that pull toward the less functional points farther "down" on the continuum. Also note that there are marks along the sides that indicate the passage of time over the life cycle, as a person's pattern of decision-making can be shown "up" and "down" from one point to another going through life.

The shading is also important. The chart shows the Middle as a light area at the top, with increased shading toward the extremes of both Magnification and Minification at the bottom on either side. This represents the increased intensity of anxiety bound up in the more rigid denial modes of Magnification (denying limitation) and Minification (denying potential) toward the two ends of the continuum.

This longitudinal chart will now be the basic one used throughout the rest of the book. However, there are some concepts that do not lend themselves to be presented in this format and are better displayed in the original perspective of the 2D version. Nonetheless, the two versions remain consistent with each other and with the overall framework.

Longitudinal

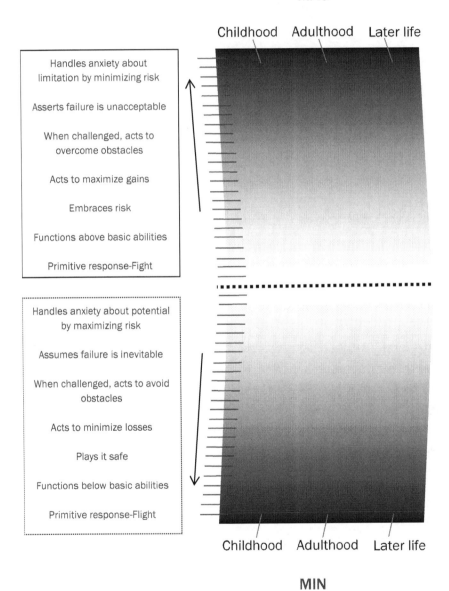

Figure 3.1

Direction and Change

To make changes in one's life using this framework, a person needs to know which way the Middle is. Too often the person from Magnification, when strenuously challenged about limitation, will re-double the effort to beat the challenge and actually move away from the Middle, even farther toward the Magnification end of the continuum. Similarly, the Minifier, under the stress of the challenge to respond with strength, will default to Minification, away from the Middle. The person operating from Magnification will tell you that you just can't let anything beat you, and the person operating from Minification will tell you that you just have to know when to give up. Both rationales make sense generally, but for each of these particular people, those assumptions validate and maintain their specific patterns of the status quo and thereby impede any efforts to change.

I often talk with people about playing the odds. Given an awareness of one's patterns in various systems in one's life, one can predict pretty well what that person's reaction will be in hypothetical situations. People understand this easily. For a go-getting Magnifier, how likely is it for her to respond to her boss's question about her slightly decreasing performance, with resignation and acceptance of her deficiency? How likely is it for the Minifier, in the same situation, to take the boss's question as a stimulus to achieve even greater levels of performance, rather than criticism?

Therefore, when I talk with people faced with a decision about some action to take, I ask them to consider making it by moving toward the Middle. There is a slight chance that the Magnifier will miss out on an opportunity, or the Minifier will be over-stepping their bounds, but most likely not. Actually, the mere fact that the person has a question about the decision typically indicates they are at a point of being able to make a change in the pattern to operate differently, but are in unfamiliar territory.

This unfamiliarity correlates precisely with the emergence of anxiety as one moves toward the Middle. The anxiety is partly about the other end of the continuum: limitation for the Magnifier and potential for the Minifier. However, it is much more about the anxiety of living in the world, because one will be vulnerable with the consequences of a decision made more toward the Middle. The Magnifier does not know what to do with the experience of actually allowing some limitation and having it go okay, or even well, and then does not know how to accept it. Was this a fluke? Do I have to keep on accepting limits? Life isn't supposed to work this way, or is it? The current experience does not make sense in terms of that person's life experience, but it does indeed seem right in some other way.

The Minifier is equally confused when they take a chance and it works out well. Things don't usually go well, so was this just a matter of good luck or was it actually a good decision? If it was based on a sound assessment of the situation, then this is not at all familiar to this person and is confusing emotionally, even when it makes sense logically.

Decision and change — Experimentation

As presented in Chapter 1, decision-making then is a way to experiment with making major changes in how one functions in various systems in one's life. Making decisions more in the direction of the Middle on the chart gives a person the ability to discover more adaptive responses to challenges as they come up, because they are based on less distortion.

Change begins with an awareness of where the Home position is on the Mag/Min continuum. Obviously you cannot know whether you have made a change if you have no starting point to compare the current behavior to. Even more important is knowing which side of the continuum one starts from, because there may indeed be a change, but it may be a regressive one, farther toward the extreme end, which means a reinforcement of the pattern, not a change in it.

Given the importance of knowing the Home position, the reader has presumably read Chapter 2 on identifying the Home position. Reading this current chapter about change may prompt a review of that chapter to confirm the original conclusion, or perhaps a re-evaluation of it. Once the Home position is established, the next step is to take the opportunity to experiment in order to practice changing the pattern of one's operating from that point of the Home position on the continuum.

Often my clients will begin to get a general sense of what needs to happen in order to get relief from their problem. Then they will ask me what they should do to change. They are frequently disappointed when I take a negative approach and tell them to focus all their energy on not yielding to the old pattern. I then add that efforts to try to actively make a change are counter-productive.

This answer comes both from my experience in working with people, and from the grounding of my work in systems theory. As mentioned in the Introduction, a major foundation for this whole Magnification/Minification framework is systems theory. This will be explained in the following chapter, but it is appropriate to introduce it here in relation to the question of how to initiate the change process.

A basic assumption in systems theory is that systems maintain themselves as they are organized in an ongoing process of balancing, often referred to as homeostasis, or the steady state. This is not a static process but a dynamic one. The system is always in motion, like gravity or the regular beating of your heart. One can detect this dynamic in a system by observing the patterns.

This Mag/Min framework can be understood as one in which a person's pattern of magnification or minification functions as part of balancing of the various systems they live in, whether it is their family, their place of employment, their neighborhood, or their social network. So a change in one's pattern of magnification or minification means a change in the balance of the system.

To initiate change, then, requires that a person have an understanding of how their own pattern of magnification or minification contributes to the balance of that system. But because change is disruptive to the steady state, people generally look first to change others and keep their own pattern intact. What happens as a consequence is that the systemic forces of balancing overwhelm this one person's attempt to change the powerful dynamics of the system and nothing changes. This validates the common notion that you cannot change others, only yourself. So then my "negative" approach to changing one's patterns is to focus on oneself and not the other.

Therefore, change requires that a person understand both the larger patterns of the system that they live in, as well as their own individual patterns, and then how these two sets of patterns go together. The more a person gains a better understanding of all of these patterns, the more grounded is their orientation in the system. As stated above, the usual tendency is to attempt to gain this orientation by focusing on the larger patterns external to one's Self. A person will attempt to understand what is going on in interactions with others by trying to figure them out while keeping one's own part in the interaction separate. This person is so argumentative. That person is so easy to get along with. My family is so dysfunctional. We all get along so well in our church. The problem in our school is this one teacher who always causes trouble. One of my kids is always concerned about my health and the others could not care less. In this book, this orientation in a system gained by keeping one's own participation in the patterns separate will be referred to as an other-focus. It means that a person seeks to gain orientation: where I fit; how this system works; and so forth by focusing primarily on other people and only secondarily on their own dynamics.

The opposite practice is referred to as self-focus. This is the effort to gain orientation in a system through a focus on one's own part in the dynamics and patterns of the system. This idea of self-focus versus other-focus will be explained more thoroughly in Chapter 4, which deals more specifically with change in systems using the concept of triangles.

Self-focus and change

The opportunity for change comes up as one is faced with a decision. As described in the Introduction, these can be big or little decisions, but the focus needs to be on the pattern of decision-making as either from the Magnification or Minification side. The beginning of change is at the point where one makes a decision that does not maintain that Mag or Min pattern, and this requires operating from a position of self-focus.

When faced with a decision to take an initiative or to decline it, the typical pattern for the person who magnifies, of course, will be to always take it, and the person who minifies always to let it go. So the possibility for change for the Magnifier is to consider the unthinkable, namely to decline, and, for the Minifier, to go for it. This does not mean that either of these different responses is actually the one they need to take. It does mean they need to seriously consider the alternative they never allow.

If that different alternative is clearly a bad idea from anyone's perspective, consideration of that choice would most likely not come up in any serious way. However, the opportunity for change occurs in those instances where it should be seriously considered, but the pattern blocks that consideration. This is precisely where the person has a sense that the risk of maintaining the old pattern may be worse than the possible consequences of change. As described in the examples at the beginning of this chapter, this is where the person realizes the need to make a change.

I never tell people whether they need to make a change. If they do need to, they already know it. The question is what to do. I tell them they need to experiment with changing the pattern of their usual responses. This notion of an experiment is important, because again it is a systemic idea. I cannot tell them what action to take to cause a specific result. They need to try out not yielding to the old pattern of magnification or minification, see what happens, and then work from there to continue the experiment as change begins to happen.

Let's take some examples and use the chart to portray the process. A Magnifier knows that his third marriage is in trouble and he is considering a divorce from his current wife. He has a sense something is wrong if he is doing it for a third time, but does not know what to do. When asked what his pattern has been in the past two break-ups, he says he just left both times and tried to make a clean break, not wanting to get into any messy encounters, leaving most of the work to the lawyers.

So for this man, the experiment would be for him to make a decision about this marriage by allowing some limitations, thereby moving more toward the Middle on the continuum. This might mean talking directly with his wife about the possibility of divorce and dealing with the limitations of a "mess" of upset feelings, lack of understanding of each other's perspectives, lack of agreement or of resolution. He always wants things "over and done with" and this approach has him struggling with the anxiety and vulnerability of having to work through a process that takes time, and challenges him to deal with himself and his part in the troubles, as well as in the resolution of them.

He would see this as an onerous effort that could only limit the ultimate outcome of getting a divorce and moving on. Except that he knows better, because he has the evidence of two previous divorces, where moving on led to exactly the same problem he started with. So the alternative, the possibility of a change in the pattern, lies in considering the unthinkable, which is to interrupt the automatic response of taking the initiative to get it over with. The concrete behaviors might be to make himself take opportunities to talk with his wife directly about divorce, instead of staying late at work, watching TV, or going to bed. It might be to not set deadlines for taking action with a lawyer, but try to "wait and see" for a while. He decides to try this approach, which is depicted in Figure 3.2. This new effort is portrayed as a move "up" toward the lighter area of the Middle.

Divorce Tracking

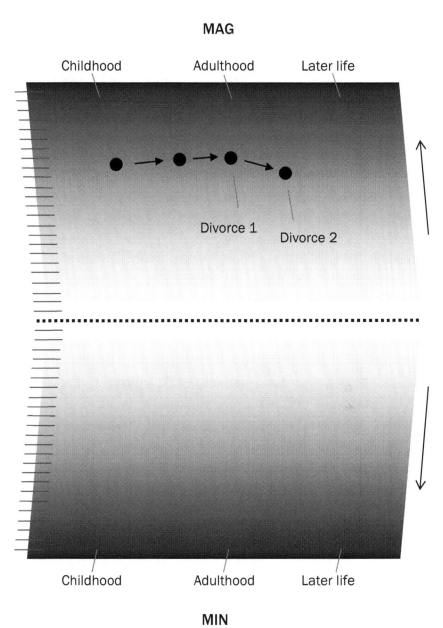

Figure 3.2

He makes this decision because he is very worried that by continuing this pattern he will end up with a series of unhappy marriages and ultimately die alone. However, to allow encounters with his wife feels very risky to him, even though at the same time he has a sense it is the right thing for him to do. He is confused about doing something so counter to his usual way of operating, that seems right but makes him anxious. This set of feelings is very characteristic of making a change in an old pattern. I work with my clients about trusting this perception of a contradiction between the feeling and the thinking as an indicator of being on the right track, not the wrong one, for making changes. The anxiety actually confirms being on the right track. It is rather more a general feeling of vulnerability than of anxiety about a specific threat.

It is important to note here that this effort is not designed with a goal of either staying married or getting divorced. The change in the pattern would result in a good decision either way about the marriage because it would have come from a thorough assessment of the situation and the options, as opposed to an automatic response from the past pattern, which would have left him not knowing if he had made a good decision, whether he stayed in the marriage or not.

Let's consider another response of a person in that same situation. He decides that this time, after two divorces, he is going handle this third failed marriage by redoubling his efforts to get rid of this marriage and find a wife that he will stay with forever. He hires a different lawyer, moves out of town to minimize contact with his third wife, and makes a fresh start. This is depicted in Figure 3.3. On the chart this is a move "down" toward the darker end of the continuum for the Magnifier.

Divorce Tracking

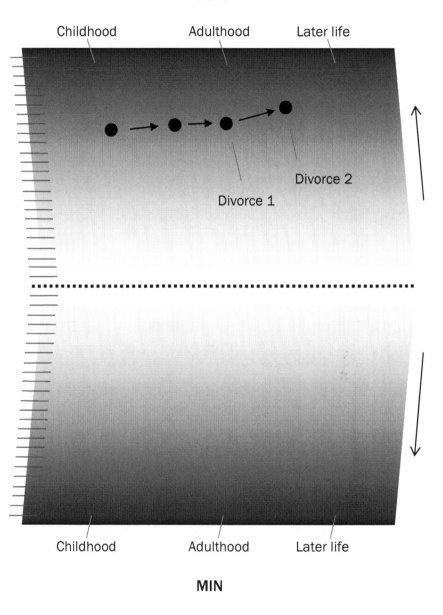

Figure 3.3

This is a change. It is a change in the intensification of the automatic response to the anxiety prompted by the problems in the marriage, moving toward a more extreme point on the continuum toward Magnification. This move intensifies the pattern but does not change it, compared to the move toward the Middle for the previous husband, who allowed more limitation.

Now for an example from the Minification side. I will use the same situation of a husband considering his third divorce. This husband has always assumed he was an inadequate husband and that his wives finally got tired of his problems and he ended up agreeing to a divorce, hoping that things would turn out better with a different woman in the future.

For him, the experiment would be to move toward the Middle by not defaulting to the limitations of his adequacies, and the futility of exploring any possibility of improving this marriage, and instead to consider not divorcing. Again, the point is not to prevent divorce or make the marriage work, but to interrupt the old pattern of minification, and see what outcomes the experiments yield, so he can then trust his decision either to divorce or stay married.

His experiment might mean initiating discussions with his wife about his unhappiness in the marriage and his thinking about divorce, instead of waiting for her to talk about her complaints. It might mean hiring a lawyer to find out about his rights before waiting for his wife to hire one, and then having to respond to her proposals. Or it might mean his looking for a marital therapist and asking his wife to come with him to see what is possible. Any of these efforts could be represented by the arrow in Figure 3.4, a move "up" toward the Middle.

Divorce Tracking

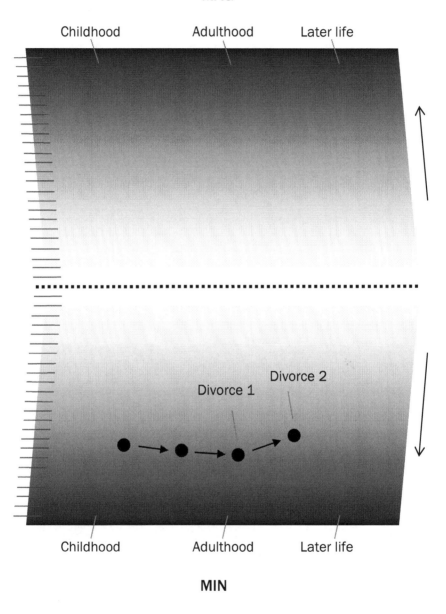

Figure 3.4

Just as for the husband operating from Magnification, this would make him very anxious, while it still makes sense as the right thing to do, because he knows there is something too familiar about going through this again for a third time without any hope of things turning out differently.

To complete the range of possible responses, it is also useful to consider the response of a minifying husband who moves farther toward the extreme of Minification. This might be a response to hire a lawyer right away and get it over with sooner, thinking this is doing it differently (same behavior as the magnifying husband moving out of town). The husband decides to admit to himself that he is indeed the problem and the honorable thing to do is to relieve his wife of the burden of him and his problems. Again, this is a change, but it is a move of intensification of the old pattern, which leads to more extreme and automatic responses, not to a change in the pattern that allows consideration of more options possible in the middle range of the continuum. This can be seen in Figure 3.5.

Divorce Tracking

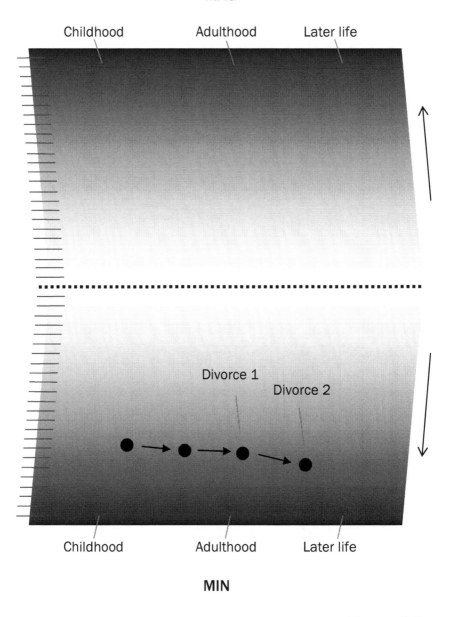

Figure 3.5

In these charts each of the husbands' Home positions is plotted on the Mag/Min continuum, and then each of their actions, based on decisions about what to do about their marriages, is plotted in reference to the original Home position, offering a graphic representation of the change, or lack of it, described in the narrative above.

To reiterate, changes toward the Middle require the practice of self-focus as one works to understand the Self and one's own patterns within the system in order to experiment with different patterns.

Figure 3.6 summarizes the scenarios above and enables the reader to see what could be assumed to be profiles of four sets of behaviors, dealing in this instance with a troubled marriage. However, the decisions about the marriage can generalize to a pattern of similar decisions and behaviors in many other areas of their lives, further validating the Home position. Perhaps you can put yourself into one of these behavioral profiles by generalizing to some of the typical decisions you make. Figure 3.7 which follows, gives you some blanks to fill in.

Profiles

MAG

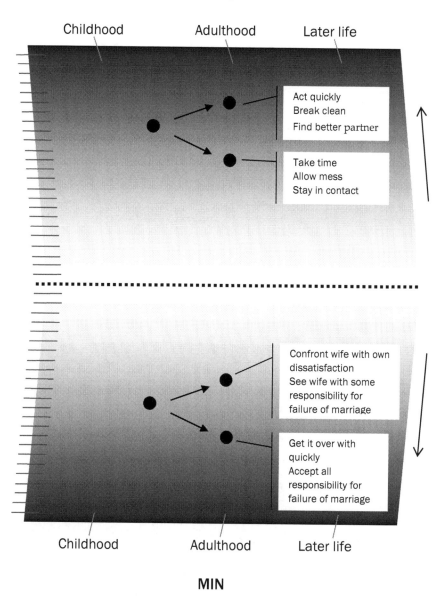

Figure 3.6

Profiles

MAG

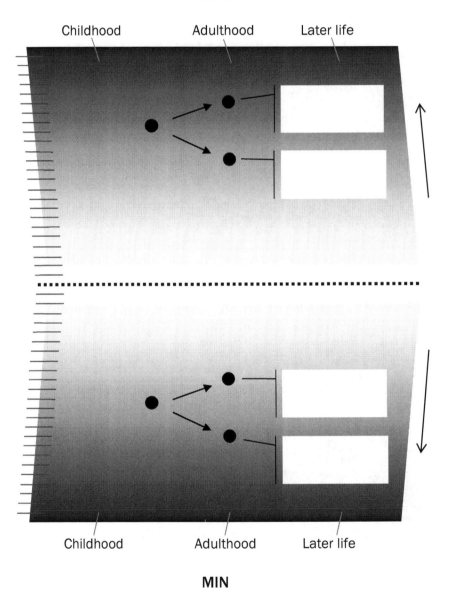

Figure 3.7

Long term change

Of course, the experiment is not finished with any of the moves described above. I often tell my clients that, while the first move takes a lot of thought and planning and courage, it is not as powerful as what comes next: one's response to the consequences of that move. The real leverage happens as you respond to your own actions and to the responses of others to your actions. The change in the pattern happens over time as one is able to move the Home position closer to the Middle. This happens as Magnifiers allow more limitation than they are used to and become more and more familiar with this new way of living life. The same happens for Minifiers as they allow more potential than they are used to.

This whole process of working to move to the Middle is based on the dynamic of Differentiation from Bowen theory. Bowen explained it this way in his seminal book *Family Therapy in Clinical Practice*:

> This concept is a cornerstone of the theory, and if my discussion becomes repetitive, I beg the reader's indulgence. The concept defines people according to the degree of *fusion* or *differentiation* between emotional and intellectual functioning. This characteristic is so universal it can be used as a way of categorizing all people on a single continuum. At the low extreme are those whose emotions and intellect are so fused that their lives are dominated by the automatic emotional system. Whatever intellect they have is dominated by the emotional system. These are the people who are less flexible, less adaptable, and more emotionally dependent on those about them. They are easily stressed into dysfunction, and it is difficult for them to recover from dysfunction. They inherit a high percentage of all human problems. At the other extreme are those who are more differentiated. It is impossible for there to be more than relative separation between emotional and

intellectual functioning, but those whose intellectual functioning can retain relative autonomy in periods of stress are more flexible, more adaptable, and more independent of the emotionality about them. They cope better with life stresses, their life courses are more orderly and successful, and they are remarkably free of human problems. In between the two extremes is an infinite number of mixes between emotional and intellectual functioning. (Bowen, p. 362, emphasis in original)

So then, the more a person is able to separate emotional from intellectual functioning to some degree, the more the person is able to make a better assessment of the probability of a favorable outcome. At higher levels of differentiation, the person does not allow anxiety to distort the decision-making process so they do not magnify or minify the assessment of the likelihood of a favorable outcome. At lower levels of differentiation, the person's assessment is driven by the anxiety, and they default to the old pattern of either magnification or minification. Change, then, in the pattern of magnification or minification, is actually a change in the level of differentiation.

It should be noted, as was explained in Chapter 2, that the work of change happens with the Basic self. As a person moves the Home position closer to the Middle, it changes the coordination with the Social self, but the level of functioning and the level of differentiation only change as the Basic self changes.

Given that change takes time and happens as the pattern changes, how much change is possible? Does it make a difference for the overall change process where the initial Home position is located on the continuum? How far can a person move on the continuum? Can a person move from the extreme of Mag or Min all the way to the Middle? Is it easier to make a move from less of an extreme Home position to the Middle because it is closer?

The simple answer to these questions is that from my experience and the theories that support this framework, change is always possible, and any change can significantly impact people's lives in positive as well as negative ways.

Consistent with Bowen theory, I would say that a large change of the Home position from far out on one of the extremes all the way to the Middle is unlikely. That is just not a reasonable expectation given the power of systemic patterns, especially multigenerational ones, that Bowen theory focuses on. Much smaller changes on the continuum toward the Middle, that are more possible, can make a major change in the lives of individual people and their families and organizations. These significant changes will however be different depending on where the Home position starts from.

Another aspect of change over the long term is what happens with the coordination between the Basic self and Social self. Figure 3.8 shows the continuum with the two selves. There are four sets of two boxes that represent the coordinated Basic and Social selves. The top row are those that are the same on either side of the continuum, and the bottom are the opposite ones. There is no significance to one row being above or below the other. Note that the arrow that designates the Home position comes from the Basic self, not the Social, because it is the Basic self that determines the primary level of functioning or the basic level of maturity. Also note that this chart lists the behaviors of Mag and Min from earlier charts, but here with the addition of self and other focus.

Basic and Social Selves
More Extreme – Less Functional

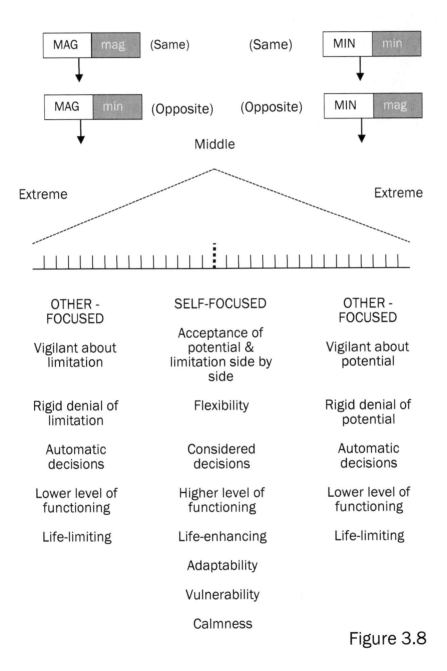

Figure 3.8

If, for example, a MAG/mag begins over time to be able to self-focus, accept more limits, and control their reactivity to act impulsively, acting in the old way socially will become more incongruent. To take charge and ignore limits will just not seem right, even if others expect it from them. In the same way, if a MIN/min begins over time to be able to self-focus, take more risks, and control their reactivity to hesitate, acting in the old way socially will become more incongruent. To hold back and decline opportunities will just not seem right, even if others expect it from them.

If the denial modes are opposite, the change in Basic self will also be matched in the Social self but in a different way. The MAG/min, by accepting limitation more, will begin to embrace the way they have acted socially. It will become more natural with the change in the Basic self. Some people have remarked that, in this situation, the Social self provides a model for how to act to implement the change in the Basic self. In a similar way, as the MIN/mag begins to actually take more initiative, it begins to fit how they have been acting socially. Essentially, change in the Basic self disrupts the previous coordination with the Social self.

Over the long term, a change of the Home position more toward the Middle means the person is operating at a higher level of functioning because they are able to handle anxiety better. However, at the more extreme points on either end of the continuum, the person lives life from a more other-focused orientation, and the Social self is more variable in different situations as it adapts to them in order to manage the anxiety and stabilize the Home position. In this way the Social self serves to maintain the coordination with the Basic and inhibit change and movement toward the Middle. This is a stable coordination of Basic and Social self at this point farther out on the continuum from the Middle, for either the Mag or Min side.

If a person makes changes in the Basic self, moving the Home position closer to the Middle, the coordination between the Basic and Social selves becomes more coherent, and decisions are more effective because there is less wasted energy with reactivity about limitation and potential. The person behaves in interactions with others more consistently with how they think, and how they think is more mature as they can weigh the probabilities of the outcome of their decisions more reasonably. Figure 3.9 simply demonstrates this change closer to the Middle.

Basic and Social Selves
Less Extreme – More Functional

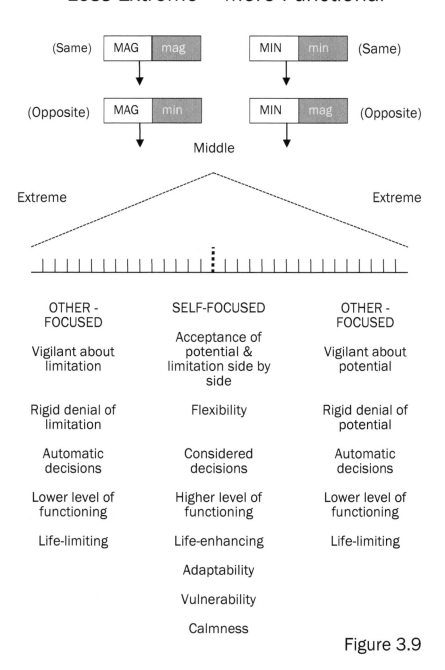

Figure 3.9

As mentioned earlier, I have deliberately omitted any scaling of discrete points on the continuum. This framework is not developed enough to be able to distinguish the functioning of a person, say, three points out from the Middle from a person five points out. Any particular points placed on the scale would be arbitrary. However, for the purposes of using this framework to make changes in one's life, it is critical to know which way the Middle is at any point in time. It is also very useful to be able to track one's changes of the pattern of decision-making over time from one area of the continuum to another so one can assess progress or regression.

In the previous longitudinal charts the shading accomplishes both these purposes. Decisions made from a "darker" point on the continuum can be distinguished from those made from a "lighter" shade without having to define that distinction in quantifiable terms. As a person gets to know their patterns and experiments with changing them, they can recognize the difference between behavior based on a decision made from the Home position farther out on the continuum from one made closer to the Middle. A person can tell the difference between more or less magnification and more or less minification (depending on which reflex one has). A person also can learn to tell the difference over time between higher and lower functioning, more or less anxiety, flexibility, vulnerability, and calmness. See Figure 0.1 again for these variables shown on the ends versus the Middle on the continuum.

Over time a person can also begin to recognize the extent or significance of changes, again without having to quantify them. Predictably, Magnifiers will have a tendency to exaggerate the extent of the changes, and Minifiers to minimize them. Not having a numerical scale reduces the possibility of this reactivity and allows for people, both Mags and Mins, to make better assessments of their changes, and thereby make further changes in the basic pattern. The Magnifiers will not make the mistake of assuming they have made more progress than they have, and then not see limitations in the future as clearly. Similarly, Minifiers will not assume they have made less progress than they have, and then not see the possibilities in the future.

Practice

Up to this point I have described the basic process of change using this framework. Simply stated, it is a process of experimenting with making decisions differently, less magnification or less minification over time, so that the pattern of decision-making changes. This change over the long term is a change in the Home position, toward the Middle on the continuum. As described in the Introduction, it is a powerful change.

However, the power of the change is lost if the overall pattern does not change. To shift the Home position requires the discipline of continued attention and effort to make decisions differently. I describe this work in Chapter 7, The Guide, as a two-phase effort. The first phase is the initial working to understand the direction of experimentation to move toward the Middle, followed by success with the change in decision-making. In the beginning, the results of the experimentation are counter-intuitive. Magnifiers have a hard time getting used to the idea that they are actually more successful and have less stress when they allow limitations, just as Minifiers have the same hard time getting used to the idea that they are more successful more often when they allow potential. Magnifiers still want to seize the opportunities and take the risks, and Minifiers still want to be cautious and be sure before taking any risks.

It takes time for either to get familiar with this different way of living life. People never get completely familiar with the difference. There will always be a pull toward the old pattern. This can probably be explained by the assumption that the reflex of Mag or Min never changes, while the response to that reflex can definitely change and thereby leverage powerful changes in one's functioning.

A person far out on the extreme of Magnification could work hard and make a significant change in allowing limitation but still be a go-getter, sometimes abrasive with friends and with an overbearing attitude. But now for the first time, he is able to listen to criticism from his employees as their boss, and has medical tests that validate his decreased risk of a heart attack. His employees would say the attitude around the office has changed a lot. However, his changes are different from a Magnifier whose Home position is initially more in a midrange position on the Magnification side of the continuum. As this person changes, allowing more limitations, his decisions to cut back his hours at work, exercise with more reasonable workouts, and spend more time with his now-teenaged children, would allow him more options for the future than his colleague farther out on the Mag continuum, who is still quite driven by work. Nevertheless, the changes are powerful for both of them and the people around them.

Of course the situation is the reverse for a Minifier. One may begin far out on the extreme with depression and thoughts of suicide and unsuccessful therapy, terrified of being okay, and end up, not a bubbling extrovert, but someone no longer dealing with chronic visits to the emergency room and able to hold a job that is not fulfilling, but is satisfactory. For that person, such a change comes at the price of very hard work and has a major impact on his life and those of the people always worried about him and taking care of him. Like the less extreme Magnifier, a person operating from Minification who begins from a less extreme Home position may make changes in the pattern of decision-making so that he finds himself in a better job with a promotion and more responsibility and with fewer discipline problems with his children.

So then, the work is the effort to continually monitor one's response to the Mag/Min reflex, both initially and then over the long term of one's life. But how does one maintain this effort?

I think of it as a practice. But it is not just practicing a technique or a skill to achieve an end goal. Rather, it is attending to the practice of living one's life differently. This is the second phase of the effort to change. Once a person has reached the point of being able to make decisions differently, the work requires the effort to maintain that change of pattern by staying on the track of making decisions on this different basis. One needs a point of anchoring or grounding.

The process of the work then is one of attending to choices as they come up, experimenting with making decisions more toward the Middle, and then having a way to assess the results of those experiments, both immediately in the short term, as well as over time, to assess whether the overall pattern is changing.

Because I am a therapist, the question comes up for me about whether this work requires that a person be in therapy. While I am very familiar with how people do this work with me in therapy, I do not think that is a requirement. What I do think is essential is: 1.) People need to develop a practice, a habitual way of doing the experimentation and assessing the results, and 2.) They need some external points of feedback to guide them in this practice.

For some, this certainly can be done with a therapist (one who works in ways that are consistent with this framework, though not necessarily using it explicitly). Others stay grounded in their work by maintaining relationships with people who do understand this framework and with whom they share their personal efforts. (An example of this kind of practice is where people work on maintaining their changes with their addictions in a network of people who understand the work of getting sober and clean.)

Many people have their own reflective practice of meditation or journaling that can incorporate this Mag/Min framework. It is also possible to use readings in this framework (which will hopefully become more abundant). Though I still think that these individual, solo practices benefit from some external points of feedback from other people.

As the presentation of this Mag/Min framework moves into this exploration of change, it eventually reaches the threshold of systems theory that underlies the whole model. Given the foundation of this model in systems theory, it has to. However, I find that people need to first grasp the dynamics of the Mag/Min continuum for an individual person, especially oneself, before adding this next layer of complexity. Systems theory explains the larger context in which each individual person, operating from Mag or Min, interacts with others from their Home positions, creating patterns at this next level of interactions, beyond the patterns for each individual person.

This is the major reason that the practice, as described above, needs to incorporate some way for people to manage the ability to stay anchored in the different pattern of decision-making. It is simply because the system of all the other people in one's family or organization, interacting together, creates a larger pattern of systemic balance that challenges the person making individual changes to work to hold their own in order to counter the pull of the larger systemic forces. More about this next level in the following chapters.

While it may seem daunting to incorporate so much complexity, it is a natural extension of thinking about this whole idea of Mag/Min because, once people have a basic understanding of the continuum and themselves, they inevitably move on to ask me about patterns *between* people.

In the next chapter I will shift the focus of the Mag/Min framework from the Self as an individual to the Self in relationship using systems theory.

Chapter 4

The Self in Relationships

Magnification/Minification is both a powerful idea and a powerful tool. As an idea it has a remarkable ability to explain people's behavior. As a tool it provides a way for people to make significant changes in their lives. However, making changes is not easy. There are two levels of change, and they must be distinguished. The first level is one of modifying the decisions one makes as they come up in various situations.

From the Minification side, a man buying a new lawn mower may remember that he often just accepts what the salesperson tells him is the best model, regardless of the cost. So this time he decides to make a change, ask some questions, and find out more about what would be a good choice, given his needs and the price. He does that and makes a choice he feels good about. He goes home and tells his wife about his purchase; she tells him he spent too much money. He says no more, goes out and mows the lawn, questioning his choice the whole time. Here's the same situation from the Magnification side. The man knows he always just decides what the right product is for him and never asks for help from a salesperson. Remembering this, he decides to make a change, and asks some questions of the salesperson about the mower. He makes a choice that fits for him, now with better information supporting that choice. He too goes home and tells his wife about his new purchase and she tells him he spent too much. He says no more, goes out and mows the lawn, thinking about how wrong she is. Both revert back to the old pattern after talking with their wives.

For the Minifier and the Magnifier, change to a new pattern in this situation, the second level of change, would be first to engage their wives in a conversation, then listen to their disagreement, while keeping focused on their own position about having made a good choice. The first level of change was to make the decision about the purchase in a different way. For both of them that was by asking for help from the salesperson. The second level of change would be to maintain that change within Self and in interaction with others. For the Minifier in this example, it would mean not immediately yielding his position about having made a good decision, just because his wife disagrees with him. For the Magnifier, it would mean not immediately dismissing his wife's disagreement because she can't be right.

At the first level, people can make changes in the decisions they make periodically, but cannot sustain them across a variety of situations. The overall pattern of decision-making does not change. This is because change at this second level requires a change of Self.

This chapter takes the presentation of the Mag/Min framework from the first to the second level of change. It does this by explaining the particular definition of Self used in this framework, which is different from the typical understanding of Self. In this book it requires understanding the Self in relationship, not as a stand-alone, autonomous being. So in this framework a person cannot change the Self without changing the set of relationships within which that Self exists.

The Self is embedded in relationships because, from this systems view of the Self, the network of relationships is essential for the very existence of the Self. That is what provides the stability we all need in order to know who we are from moment to moment and throughout a lifetime of aging. To not have a stable sense of Self is terrifying. Actually this stability works so well that people seldom question it. Most of the time, most people never think about who they are. We are generally well protected from this terror. However, there are times when people do question who they are, often as they struggle with losses and suffering, which can become a crisis precisely because they lose this stability.

A husband who loses his wife after 35 years of marriage may well have trouble managing his life alone, as he no longer has the marriage and his partner to give his life meaning. So now he is not so sure of who he is. A soldier returning from combat with PTSD may find himself confused about who he is, as he feels very alienated from his family, who loves him but cannot get close to him, because he cannot let them. Or a 16-year-old girl being sexually abused by her father is confused about her identity, as she feels the shame and hurt of having a major part of who she is violated. Each of these people has lost control of their identity, which they need in order to understand themselves and present who they are to the world.

Their anxiety about who they are reveals the critical importance of the Self as a stabilizing factor for living in systems of relationships with others. But these are examples where the Self is threatened as a result of external circumstances. What about the situation of intentionally choosing to change one's own pattern of decision-making, which then changes the Self?

To change the Self deliberately involves disrupting this stability, which is so important for our well-being. That is why change at this second level on the one hand is so challenging, and on the other can be so rewarding. All of this needs to be explained further.

To begin with, the presentation of Magnification/Minification so far has been all in terms of one person. The framework does work well as it describes the functioning of an individual. You probably have been able to apply it to yourself. However, once people begin to understand it, they start to ask broader questions about relationships. Frequently they will ask where these dynamics of magnification and minification come from. Do they begin in childhood? Are you born with them? If your parent has a Home position on one side, does that mean you will be the opposite or the same? What about couples? Is it a better marriage if both are Mag or Min or opposite? These are very appropriate questions that reflect the sense people have about their Self being part of something bigger. The fact that they begin to ask these questions, after gaining a basic understanding of the individual's patterns of decision-making, indicates the need for this framework to be able to incorporate this larger and influential context of relationships. And it does.

Actually, with this expansion, the Magnification/Minification framework becomes more powerful as the perspective broadens to include the functioning of the larger networks of other human beings that an individual lives in. The framework does not change, but takes on deeper and broader dimensions as the magnifying or minifying patterns of one person are understood as only a part of larger patterns of their family, community, organizations, and so forth.

The Self

People have an intuitive sense of their own Self, but would be hard pressed to define it. Many thinkers have had a lot to say over the centuries about the Self, but the average person knows what their Self is. So what is it? I will define it explicitly in the next chapter, but here I want to first describe it. It is your identity. It is who you think you are, and who others think you are. It is who you and others recognize as you. It is what your name identifies. It is not the same as your body, though it includes your body. It is who you see when you look in the mirror.

This description is simple enough, but there is a complication, because there are multiple dimensions of the Self. People in different areas of your life may know different parts of you. People who knew you as a youth may say that you are still the same person, or they may say you have changed as you have aged. A tragedy or good fortune may have altered you to the point that you do not seem to be the same person. At times you or others may say you are just not "yourself."

Yet people still have a sense that, underneath it all, something stays the same. People have a sense of a kind of core Self that does not change. If this is true, how does it stay the same? There is a conflict in reconciling the sense of a core, unchangeable Self with a Self that is different in different situations and changes over time through particular experiences and aging. Which is it, fixed or changeable?

My resolution of this dilemma is to think of the Self as "stable." To understand the stability of the Self, I find it productive to expand the perspective to recognize that the Self exists in a complex network, not as a stand-alone entity. This changes the exploration from one of drilling down deep to find a core Self, instead to looking below the surface to understand the Self as part of a network. It is more of a horizontal orientation than a vertical one. Think of trees in a forest. If you dig beneath the surface, you find that the trunks of all the individual trees expand out into a wide network of roots that support each tree but also form an ecosystem that supports all the trees.

This is not really a new idea. Centuries ago John Donne captured it in his famous phrase from Devotion XVII: "No man is an island." (Donne, 1975, p. 87). In the conceptualization of the Self in this book, no Self exists all by itself. This means more than the idea that people need other people to survive. It means more than the idea that humans need the connections of family and community for physical and emotional sustenance. It means that the Self cannot exist at all outside of the network of other Selves. The body may exist independently of other people, but the Self cannot. Once people understand this framework, and can apply it to themselves, they begin to ask about their relationships with other people, and how the dynamics work when others have the same or different Home positions as Magnifier or Minifier. They recognize at some level that the Self is not really so independent. So now we need to explore this framework of Mag/Min as it operates in relationships with others. The next section of this chapter describes the patterns of interactions of the Self in a network, based on people operating from Magnification and from Minification. It is easiest to do that by starting with patterns in dyads, which is a relationship between two people. Then I will proceed to the more complex network of three dyads, a triangle.

Dyads

There are three possible dyadic relationships of Mag and Min. One is where both people are Magnifiers (Mag-Mag). Another is where both are Minifiers (Min-Min). The third is where one is a Magnifier and the other is a Minifier (Mag-Min). At this point, the reader can probably speculate fairly accurately about the typical interactions that occur in each of these different dyads. My students quickly recognize the different patterns of each dyad and offer examples from their lives. It is a very intuitive idea. The fact that these patterns are intuitive, and people recognize them quickly, is a reflection of the stability of these patterns of interaction between each person in the dyad. However, this stability of interacting with the other person also stabilizes the Self for both people in the dyad.

In the Mag-Mag relationship, there is a focus on doing what it takes to achieve a goal, and any limitation is a challenge to be overcome, not a reality to accept. Both people will share that assumption and work together to achieve goals and monitor the other for failing, if they allow any limitation. In the Min-Min relationship, there is a focus on the obstacles to achieving a goal where potential is desirable but unrealistic. Both people will share that assumption and work together to do the best they can to achieve the goal, but end up agreeing that it is really not possible to fully achieve it. In the Mag-Min relationship, the focus on a goal leads to conflict, where one person (Mag) assumes the goal is achievable and the other (Min) assumes it is not. As they work together, the conflict in their assumptions about the possibilities of achieving the goal shapes their interactions.

As explained in the previous chapters about the location of the Home position on the continuum, what determines the functionality of these patterns of interactions is not whether they are of one kind or another (Mag-Mag, Min-Min, or Mag-Min), but how mature the people are that comprise each relationship. It all depends on how far out the Home positions are on the continuum. It is also important to realize that stability does not equal functionality. The dyad can stabilize the Selves of both people at a high level of functioning or at a low level.

For example, two Mags in relationship may be very successful in meeting goals, as they each have a Home position closer to the Middle on the continuum. They assume success is possible, but have the ability to accept limits when the situation calls for it. With less mature Magnifiers, farther out on the continuum, they too assume success is possible and are actually not as successful in the end, because they cannot accept limits and instead take unnecessary risks that lead to failure over the long term. They reinforce the dynamic of magnification as it stabilizes the dyad and both individual Selves.

Similarly, two mature Minifiers, oriented more toward reasonable and limited goals, can get as much accomplished as the mature Mag-Mag pair because they take calculated risks. Two less mature Minifiers accept limits too easily and end up sabotaging their achievement of possible goals. They end up as unsuccessful as the Mag-Mag pair who ignores limitations. Again, for both the more and less mature pair, the minification stabilizes their relationship and both individual Selves.

Two teachers teaching at the same grade level in different classrooms in an elementary school in a poor neighborhood are determined to make sure their students learn, despite the difficult family backgrounds the children come from. With both teachers operating from Magnification but closer to the Middle on the continuum, they do their lesson plans carefully, creatively thinking of what can engage the students, but at the same time planning for how to handle some students coming to school angry, or not at all, or students disrupting the class and ruining the lesson plans for that day. Two less mature teachers also work hard and plan for a very good class, but do not plan for major disruptions. When the day goes well, their classes go well, but when they don't, these teachers try harder, by pushing through the agenda, having to enforce more stringent discipline to maintain order, to the point of sending students out of class and not being effective with the rest of the class.

Two parents who operate from the Minification side and are mature, have to deal with their teenage daughter, their oldest child, arguing with them to let her stay out later at night on weekends now that she is older. As Minifiers, both these parents are inclined to accede to her arguments, based on the idea that she is getting older and needs more independence. But because they operate closer to the Middle on the continuum, they are able to talk it through with each other and recognize that it is also important for them to be strong with their daughter through this developmental stage so she can learn how to deal with responsibility as well as freedom. They decide to let her have a moderately later curfew, but much less than she had wanted.

Two less mature minifying parents, dealing with the same situation, decide to accede to their daughter's requested curfew extension, agreeing that it is not worth fighting with teenagers because you can't win anyway. Over time the conflicts become more numerous and intense as the daughter keeps pushing the limits.

In the Mag-Min relationship the conflict of assumptions about possible success is no less determinative of actual success than in either of the other pairings. Again it depends on the level of maturity of the participants. With higher levels of maturity in the Mag-Min relationship, the Mag will be oriented to the possibilities of what they can achieve, and the Min will recognize the limits. Their conflict then is functional, as the Magnifier can hear the reasonable need to accept limits presented by the Minifier, and the Minifier can allow the necessary risks to trust the possibilities of succeeding presented by the Mag. The Mag-Min dynamic stabilizes the dyad and the Selves at this higher level of functioning. At lower levels of maturity, this conflict impedes success, because the conflict stabilizes the dyad and both individual Selves at this lower level of functioning. The Magnifier insists on the possibilities and sees the Minifier person as an obstacle. Conversely, the Min sees the Mag as unrealistic and needing to be stopped. They end up just as unsuccessful as the Mag-Mag and Min-Min pairs at the same levels of maturity.

An example of the Mag-Min dyad is two lovers who are trying to decide about getting married. The Magnifier proposes and is eager to get married. He sees the benefits of living together, buying a house, and wants to begin to have a family. His fiancée is not sure this is the right time because she is concerned about the security of both of their jobs, and whether she is ready to become a mother with all the responsibilities. They talk about it a lot and decide they will get married, but set the date for a year in the future, which is a compromise for both of them.

The less mature couple goes back and forth trying to decide. The man proposes and is excited, but then gets angry when his fiancée says she is not ready. She gets mad at him, feeling pressured. They both feel bad about this conflict because they do love each other, but have trouble resolving the dilemma of both wanting to get married but not being able to decide on doing it.

With all of these dyadic patterns, each person derives stability from the interaction. Each person knows who they are from interacting with the other. In the Mag-Mag dyad, each one's behavior and thinking about potential reinforces their mutual identification. Who they are as a Self is the same as the other. The more they interact, the stronger and more stable that sense of Self. The same is true for the Min-Min dyad. However, in the Mag-Min opposite dyad, each one knows who they are precisely because they are not the other.

One complication of this analysis of Mag-Min dyad patterns needs to be addressed here before moving on. It concerns the two aspects of Self, the basic and the social, each of which can be understood as operating from Magnification or Minification. As you remember from Chapter 2 on identification of the Home position and Chapter 3 on change, the Basic self is the primary one, as it determines one's behaviors and decision-making. The Social self of Magnification or Minification shapes one's social interactions, but always yields to the denial mode of the Basic self when challenged. Another factor that supports the conceptualization of the Basic as primary is the very stable coordination between them. So whether the Social is the same or opposite, the Social supports the Basic consistently through the process of coordination. However, introducing these two dimensions of Basic and Social here, into the analysis of the patterns of interaction between two people in a dyad, creates a large number of permutations of possible combinations, like a MAG/mag with a MAG/min; a MIN/min with a MIN/mag, and so on. While it may be very useful in the future for a researcher to ultimately develop the framework to that level of complexity, it is not necessary for our purposes here. It is entirely sufficient to understand the patterns in dyads of just the Basic self, regardless of whether the Social is the same or opposite.

Thus, whether a person is MAG/mag or MAG/min, they need to consider their interactions with others on the basis of operating from Magnification and determine the Basic self of the other person in the dyad in order to manage themselves in the relationship. Similarly, if a person is MIN/min or MIN/mag, they need to consider their interactions with others on the basis of operating from Minification and determine the Basic self of the other person in the dyad in order to manage themselves in the relationship. This is not at all to say that identification of the Social for oneself or others is unimportant. It can be very helpful, as explained in previous chapters, to know what one's Social self is, both to be able to support the identification of the Basic as the same or opposite, and to work with how the coordination changes with the changes in the Basic self as just explained in Chapter 3. It can also be useful to understand the behavior of others, especially if their Social is opposite of their Basic. But it is not necessary to consider all the different patterns of interactions of one's Social self with the Social selves of others, especially as one begins to consider larger systems as we will do next.

So, even with this simplification, this whole idea of the Self gaining stability in patterns paired with one other person is just the beginning of the conceptualization of the Self operating in a network of many selves. The next step is to move to a perspective of a whole network of dyads, all interacting and creating patterns where one person's Self in a dyad stabilizes that dyad, as well as other relationships in the network of a family or an organization. One way to initiate that exploration is with the concept of triangles.

Triangles

In his theory, Murray Bowen conceptualized this next level of stability of the Self, beyond dyads, in his core concept of triangles. It is outside the scope of this book to fully elaborate the concept of triangles, but the following paragraphs will first briefly describe how triangles work generally, and then describe the dynamics of triangles specifically in terms of Mag and Min. This will provide the reader with the broader perspective of the Self as existing and maintaining itself in the operations of a large network of interactions with other humans.

The basic assumption from Bowen theory is that a dyad is unstable under stress and that a triangle stabilizes the dyad. Michael Kerr summarizes the dynamics well in his comprehensive description in *Family Evaluation*:

> The triangle describes the dynamic equilibrium of a three-person system. The major influence on the activity of a triangle is anxiety. When it is low, a relationship between two people can be calm and comfortable. However, since a relationship is

easily disturbed by emotional forces within it and from outside, it usually does not remain completely comfortable very long. Inevitably, there is some increase in anxiety that disturbs the relationship equilibrium. A two-person system may be stable as long as it is calm, but since that level of calm is very difficult to maintain, a two-person system is more accurately characterized as unstable. When anxiety increases, a third person becomes involved in the tension of the twosome, creating a triangle. This involvement of a third person decreases anxiety in the twosome by spreading it through three relationships. The formation of three *interconnected* relationships can contain more anxiety than is possible in three separate relationships because pathways are in place that allow the shifting of the anxiety around the system. This shifting reduces the possibility of any one relationship emotionally "overheating." The ability to spread and shift tension, as well as to contain more of it, means that a triangle is more flexible and stable than a two-person system. (Kerr, p. 135, emphasis in original)

The triangle then achieves stability by balancing the relationship of the original twosome as the inside position and the person triangled in as the outside position. Because there are three relationships in a triangle, the outside person has two outside relationships, one with each of the other two, who have an inside relationship with each other. I depict the inside position relationship with a solid line and the outside position relationships with a broken line. See Figure 4.1.

Basic Triangle

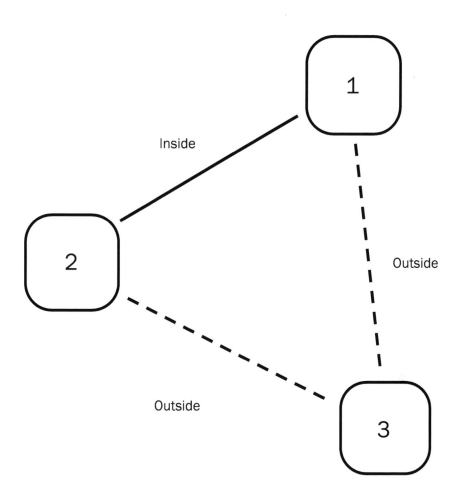

Figure 4.1

It is not healthier to be in either the outside or the inside position, because inside and outside are just the dynamics of how a triangle balances and provides stability, and do not indicate a more functional position. The balance and stability occur because the system of the triangle is constantly in motion. Sometimes I think of this process as being like trying to look two people in the eye at the same time. It is not possible. You have to look at one (leaving the other in the outside position) and then the other, even a second later, now leaving the other in the outside position. The stability comes not from inside or outside, but from the constant looking back and forth. And each of the other two is doing the same thing. Dysfunction occurs when there is a triangle that balances with a rigid pattern of one person always in the outside or the inside position. In my image, it is dysfunctional because the ability to make eye contact with either person is restricted or not possible when it is necessary. This restriction occurs because of the powerful dynamics of the triangle. This set of relationships is very stable, but this stability can cost functionality.

So when people in a dyad manage the anxiety in the relationship by triangling in a third person, they are focusing on a person outside themselves. Another element of Bowen theory directly relevant to the concept of triangles is this difference between self-focus and other-focus which was presented initially in Chapter 3 and is developed further here. As explained in the first part of this chapter, the stability of the Self gives us an intuitive and very functional sense of our identity as a person in the world, separate from other people. With the assumption that a person lives in the world deeply embedded in many relationships with the physical world, depending for survival on air and water for example, as well as relationships with other people, and that this ecology is a system of many systems that all interact constantly to maintain balance that provides stability, the question that comes up is: what does one focus on to survive, the "independent" Self or the rest of the world?

Bowen developed the idea that one could distinguish higher and lower levels of functioning in an individual person by how much they managed the anxiety of living in the world by focusing primarily and continually on the world outside of their Self, which he described as an "other-focus." The more a person managed the Self with an other-focus, the lower the level of functioning. Conversely, the more a person could stay grounded in a sense of who they are, while recognizing the patterns of the systems they operate in and function as part of the process of the balancing of those systems, the higher the level of functioning. This he contrasted as a "self-focus."

I sometimes use a gyroscope as an image to demonstrate how a person gains stability of Self through self-focus in a system. A gyroscope is a device used in vehicles like aircraft and ships for navigation to maintain orientation as the vehicle moves through air and water. It is essentially a top that spins within two rings and thereby maintains its balance as the whole mechanism resists external forces that can disrupt the orientation of the operator in space.

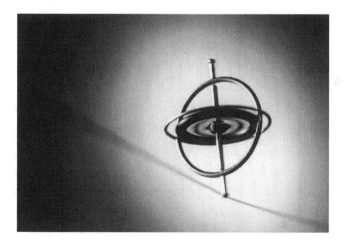

I present the idea that the whole gyroscope is the Self and that a person can maintain orientation and stability in a system by attending to the constant spinning of the inner top which maintains the balance of the whole mechanism, as the system exerts various forces on the Self. To focus primarily on the outer ring leads to attempts to balance and stabilize the Self by continually adapting to the various external forces of the system without monitoring the spinning of the inner top.

An important clarification needs to be made here, which is that a self-focus is not a focus on the Self to the exclusion of the systems that this Self is embedded in. It is not a notion of selfishness or narcissism. The distinction has to do with the priority of this focus. The person who focuses on the world outside whenever challenged by events in life, and seldom is able to see their Self as part of the dynamics of relationships they are involved in, is primarily other-focused. This is the person who blames others most of the time for the problems in their life (a Magnifier with a Home position farther out from the Middle). It is also the person who blames themselves for the problems in their life, because they are focused on how difficult the world outside them is to deal with (a Minifier with a Home position farther out from the Middle). Higher functioning Magnifiers could recognize their part in contributing to the problem in the relationship by acknowledging their avoidance of limitations (self-focus), and higher functioning Minifiers could recognize their part in contributing to the problem in the relationship by acknowledging their avoidance of potential (self-focus).

Triangles are more functional the more each of the three people is able to self-focus. The more people in the triangle manage the anxiety in the dyads by focusing on the other, the less functional is the triangle. In my eye-contact image, people function better the more they can make eye contact with the person they know they need to deal with.

A mother and father will talk about their daughter's problems in school, putting their daughter in the outside position and shifting the focus away from their spousal relationship; a worker will complain about her boss to a co-worker, aligning herself in the inside position with the co-worker, avoiding dealing with the boss directly herself, thus putting the boss in the outside position; an awkward teenage boy will say something stupid with two girls to distance himself from their excitement in talking about boys, thereby putting himself in the outside position.

Triangles are not dysfunctional in and of themselves. They always occur. It is the level of maturity of the three people in the triangle that determines the functionality of this stability, not the triangle itself. A dyad with two people of a high level of maturity will incorporate a third party to stabilize that dyad, and those three relationships can work well enough so that each person feels comfortable in each of their relationships and does not need to work harder just to maintain that stability. Each person can relate to the others in the triangle with some understanding of their part in the dynamics of their relationships with one another. Therefore, it is comfortable for any of the three to be in either the inside or outside position, because it depends on what is appropriate for the set of circumstances at the time. With lower levels of maturity, people in the dyads will be less secure about their place in the triangle and will try to relieve their anxiety by focusing on the others in their relationships to try to change the other or adapt to the other, but not look to themselves to see their part and what they need to do. As they continually overreact with more of an other-focus, they do maintain the stability of the triangle, but with less functional behaviors.

In Figure 4.2 the top diagram depicts a more flexible triangle where there is a greater probability of anyone being in either the inside or outside position depending on the situation. The lower diagram depicts a pattern of interaction in which one person is always in the outside position and the other two are always in the inside position, regardless of the situation. Both triangles are stable as they have a balance, but at different levels of functioning.

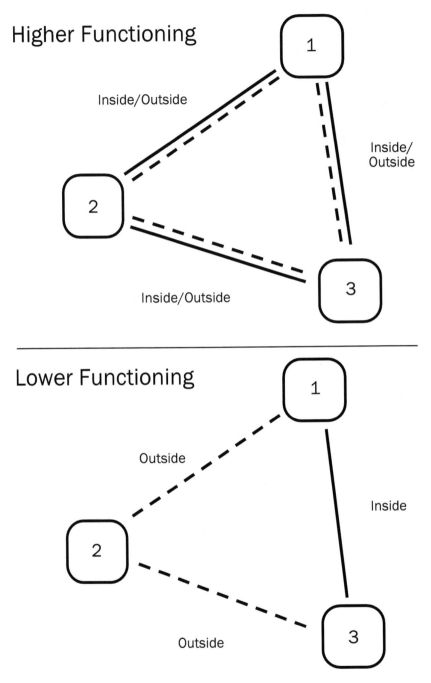

Figure 4.2

It takes a period of time for the interactions of an initial dyad triangling in a third party to develop patterns that stabilize all the dyads into a triangle. The person triangled in may end up in the outside position as the initial dyad maintains the inside relationship position, thus leaving the third party in the outside position to maintain all three dyads, or the person from the initial dyad may side with the newcomer, and the triangle then ends up stabilized with the other person from the initial dyad in the outside position maintaining all three dyads. As the patterns develop over time, the roles of the people in the inside and outside positions become more or less fixed depending on the maturity of the people in the triangle

So what does it take to reduce the rigidity of the roles in the triangle and increase the level of functioning of the people in it? The two important factors in assessing the functionality of triangles are the amount of tension in the relationships, and the level of maturity of the individuals involved. One could characterize the interaction of these two factors generally in the following way. If the level of maturity of the individuals is low, but the amount of anxiety is also low, then people can get away with behaviors that do not disrupt their lives so much. On the other hand, if the tension in the system is high, their relative immaturity creates major problems in their getting along with each other and in the larger world as well. If the level of maturity is relatively high, then low stress in the system is handled easily, with behaviors that function well as people can achieve their goals. If the stress is high with more mature people, problems occur, but they can handle them without disruptions that erode relationships.

Bowen's assertion, based on his research and the experience of Bowen theory practitioners over the years, is that the dysfunction of triangles is significantly reduced if a third person in the triangle can do two things. One is to maintain neutrality in the relationship between the twosomes that have become uncomfortable (anxious) with each other. This obviously means not taking sides, but the second task is to remain actively engaged with them while maintaining that neutrality. To attempt to be neutral by withdrawing, so as not "to get involved" actually ends up supporting the dysfunction of the triangle by staying in the outside position. This effort to stay neutral and engaged is called detriangling.

Now let us use the Mag/Min framework as the elements of the dynamics of the triangle. The following examples are organized by the possible initial dyads of the same or opposite Home positions (Mag-Mag, Min-Min, Mag-Min) and the possible combinations of triangling in a Mag or a Min into each of those initial dyads.

Mag–Mag-Mag Triangles

In the case of an initial Mag-Mag dyad, when those two triangle in another person, how that triangle gets stabilized depends on whether the person triangled in operates from Magnification or Minification. If the person triangled in is a Magnifier, all three of them are oriented to success, averse to the consideration of limits. The interactions of these three people will be oriented toward achieving goals, and that will then characterize the stability of the triangle, which reflects both the stability of each of the three dyads and of each Self within each dyad. How successful they are in achieving their goals over the long term depends on the level of maturity of the people in the triangle. At lower levels, with more other-focus, they will continually press forward, ignoring warning signs about critical limitations, and end up failing, but not changing the automatic responses to avoid limits in the decision-making. This lack of change in response to circumstances that warn of danger is exactly how this triangle maintains its stability. It is dysfunctional but the pattern is stable. To consider limits would disrupt this stability.

In a triangle of three Mags with more mature participants the interactions will still be strongly oriented to achievement of goals, but here, with more self-focus, there is the possibility of considering limitations in circumstances where there are warning signs. This more flexible pattern, where limitations can be considered, is the stability of this triangle. It is still oriented completely to potential, but with more ability to adapt to the need for limitation, because the stability is based on a wider range of possible responses than the narrow range in the triangle with people of lower maturity. This more flexible stability derives from the individual participants in the triangle operating from a Home position on the Magnification side of the Mag/Min continuum that is closer to the Middle, not as far out on the extreme as participants in the triangle with the more rigid stability. It is important to clarify here how, in spite of the fact that each of the three individuals is a Magnifier, there are still the basic dynamics of a triangle with inside and outside positions. Those positions are not defined by the differences in Home positions, because they are the same, but rather by how they align given the same Home positions. The following are two examples of these two triangles of three Magnifiers, the first one functional and the other dysfunctional.

If one of two mature, magnifying teachers turns to a third teacher, also mature and also a Magnifier, to ask her advice about doing a particular project with her class that her other colleague thinks is too difficult for the students, that outside person may agree that it is too challenging. They discuss back and forth whether the fact that only some of the class has mastered the basic skills required, and how that may frustrate and bore the others, is a serious problem. In the end the teacher with the question decides to forego the project at this time, knowing she can trust her colleague's advice because she has been supportive of other ideas from this teacher in the past. The teacher from the original pair, now in the outside position, does not feel threatened by her colleague consulting with the other teacher. The three of them have good relationships and this triangle of all Magnifiers can regulate itself to recognize and act on the need for limits, still with the Home position of Magnification. See Figure 4.3.

Higher Functioning

Teachers

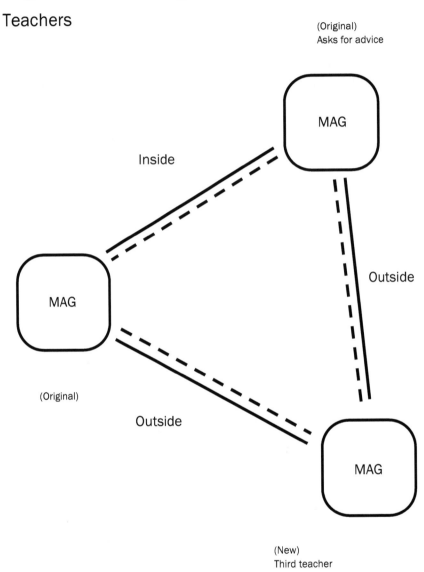

(Original)
Asks for advice

MAG

Inside

MAG

Outside

(Original)

Outside

MAG

(New)
Third teacher

Figure 4.3

Given the same situation with three teachers, but operating at lower levels of maturity, one teacher asks the magnifying colleague for advice about her project, saying she wonders if it is too challenging for the class and the teacher, initially in the outside position but now triangled in, quickly says it is not. The teacher from the original pair is a little insulted that her colleague had to get another opinion when she had already told her it would not be problem for the class, because the students with the required skills would be strong and show the others how to do it. They all end up agreeing to ignore the limits of possible problems with the reactions of the students who are not prepared for the difficulty of this project. However, there is tension in the relationships in the triangle because the teacher from the original twosome is now in the outside position, as her original colleague accepted the validation of her initial assertion from the outside teacher. See Figure 4.4.

Lower Functioning
Teachers

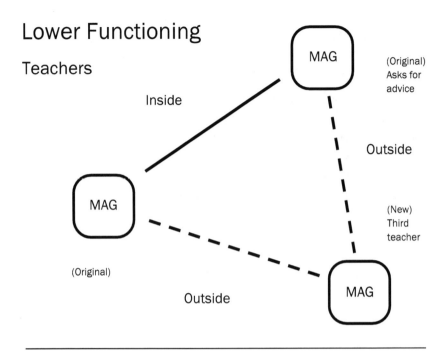

MAG

(Original)
Asks for
advice

Inside

Outside

MAG

(New)
Third
teacher

(Original)

Outside

MAG

Shift

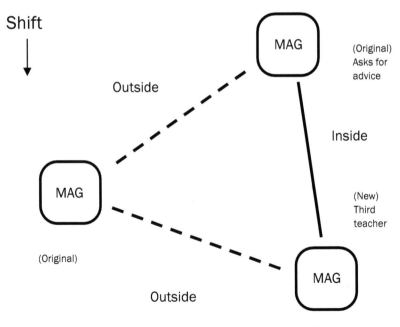

MAG

(Original)
Asks for
advice

Outside

Inside

MAG

(New)
Third
teacher

(Original)

Outside

MAG

Figure 4.4

At this lower level of maturity with a triangle of three Magnifiers, no one can accept the need for limits, and the assumptions about constantly taking risks to achieve goals leads to a stability of cycles of ups and downs, probably with the original teacher most often in the outside position. They constantly press on in spite of setbacks that they do not learn from. This is not a functional triangle and the three people are not successful over time, but the pattern is predictable, reflecting the stability of the triangle, and therefore of the Self for each individual in the triangle.

Min–Min–Min Triangles

When an initial dyad of two Minifiers triangles in a person from the Minification side, that triangle of Minifiers will stabilize around a fear of achievement. This stabilizes all three dyads and each individual's operating from Minification. How functional the triangle is depends on how much those individuals can take risks and allow for potential. Again it is a matter of how much each person can self-focus to understand their reactivity about yielding to the pattern of minifying.

When two Minifiers at a higher level of maturity triangle in another Minifier, they function well together, as they are very realistic about the necessity of limits and caution, but know enough not to be so careful that they are unable to take initiative and get things done. At lower levels, triangling in a third Minifier reinforces the overreactions to the possibilities of success, and if any one of them begins to take initiative, the stability of the triangle will force sabotage of that initiative.

A gay couple of two Minifiers are in a committed relationship and have a social network that includes other gay men. Among other things, the two partners share a strong interest in good food and cooking. They often have parties and invite friends over for dinner. One friend, another Minifier, is close with both partners. The two minifying partners know that sometimes they hold themselves back from trying new dishes. Partner 2 thinks he would like to try something new for their next party, so he asks their friend to come over and help them prepare a new recipe.

The friend presents some ideas that are not too outrageous, and Partner 2 likes them but feels cautious about the risk of failing. The friend has similar concerns, but knows that while the couple always provides good food, it is often a lot of the same or similar dishes. So he suggests this new dish, along with some old standby hors d'oeuvres and desserts as a backup. Partner 1 is now in the outside position, as the friend and his partner develop this plan. They include him but then go on to prepare it with him in a helping role.

At higher levels of functioning, Partner 2 and the friend are in the inside position as they work on preparing the new dish. Partner 1 is appropriately in the outside position because of this activity. He does not feel threatened, and as the other two introduce this new dish, all three minifiers take a risk in doing something new.

As time goes on, in the higher functioning triangle, the friend becomes a more frequent part of planning and preparing the couple's parties, as they cautiously try new food and sometimes the triangle shifts so that the couple comes up with new ideas and sometimes Partner 1 does so with the friend. The triangle of all three relationships stabilizes around a more functional flow of inside and outside positions and they increase the repertoire of recipes. See Figure 4.5.

Higher Functioning

Partners

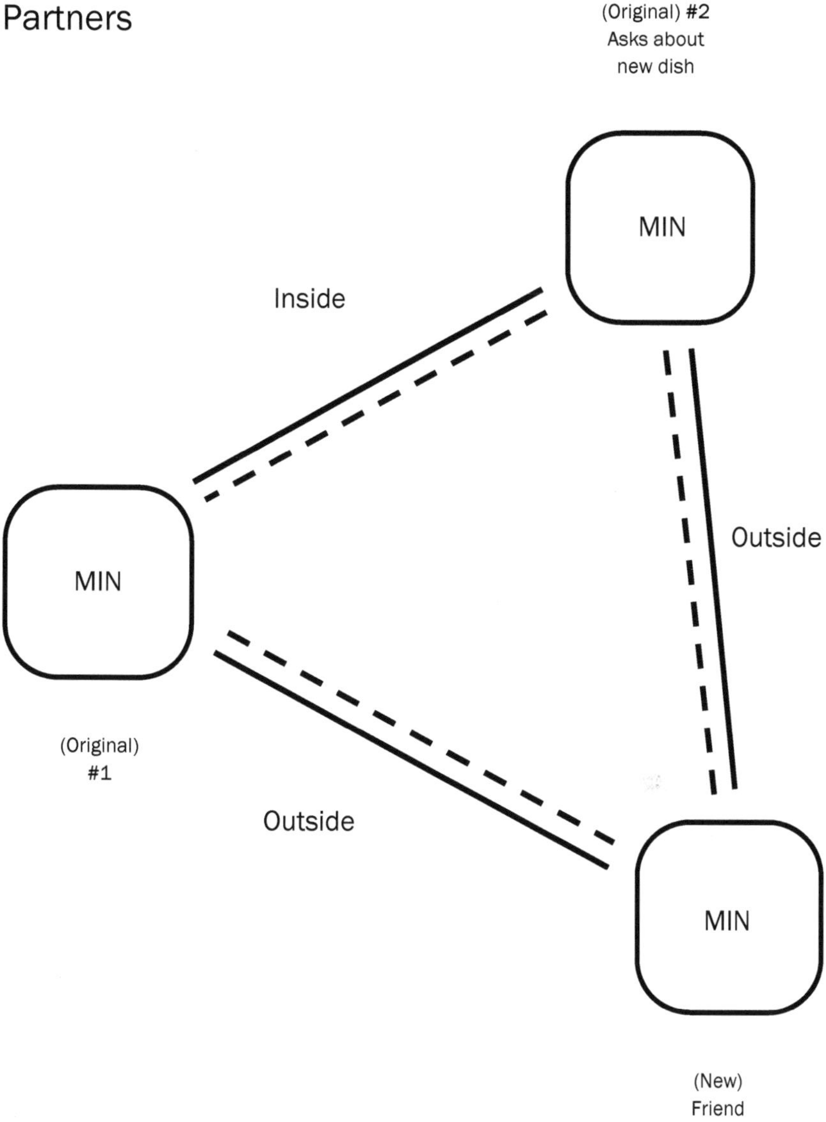

Figure 4.5

In the lower functioning triangle, Partner 2 continues to ask the friend to help with new recipes, and begins to side more and more with the friend about his proposals as Partner 1 feels more anxious about the threat of failure and the powerlessness of being in the outside position. As he continues to try to insert himself in the relationship of his partner and the friend, he ends up with conflict with both of them about trying new things, reinforcing the stability of the triangle with him in the outside position. As a result they do not experiment with new recipes but continue making the old ones, thus maintaining the established pattern. See Figure 4.6.

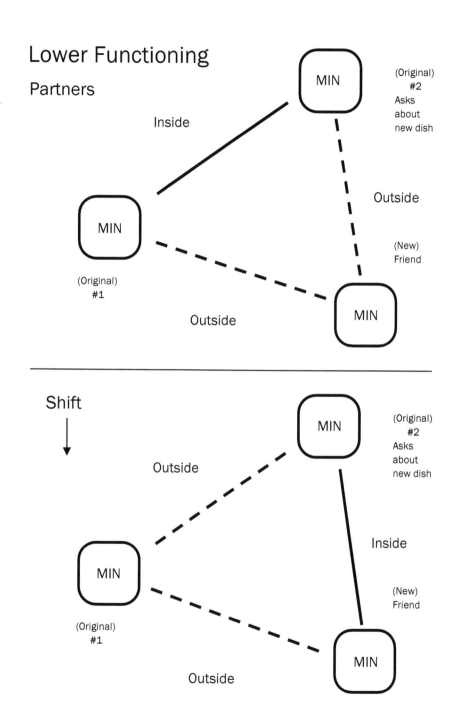

Lower Functioning

Partners

(Original) #2
Asks about new dish

Inside

Outside

(New) Friend

(Original) #1

Outside

Shift

Outside

(Original) #2
Asks about new dish

Inside

(New) Friend

(Original) #1

Outside

Figure 4.6

Mag-Mag-Min and Min-Min-Mag Triangles

In triangles with initial dyads of two Mags or two Mins, the interactions will be different if they triangle in a person from the opposite position. If two Mags triangle in a Minifier, the dynamics of the triangle will depend on whether the two Mags draw this person in and then align with each other and leave the Min in the outside position, or whether one of the Mags aligns with the Min and leaves the other Mag in the outside position. Similarly if the two Mins triangle in a Mag, it will be different depending on whether the Mins side with each other or one of the Mins sides with that Mag, leaving the Min from the initial dyad in the outside position.

In a restaurant, the owner and the manager, both Mags, are concerned about one of the servers, a Min, who generally does not turn tables over as fast as most of the other servers. She brings the food efficiently, but spends time throughout the meal talking with the customers, getting to know them, explaining the menu and checking on their reactions to the food. Both the owner and manager agree she needs to be confronted, and so the manager tells her she needs to move the process along more quickly, putting her in the outside position (Figure 4.7).

Two Mags/One Min

Restaurant

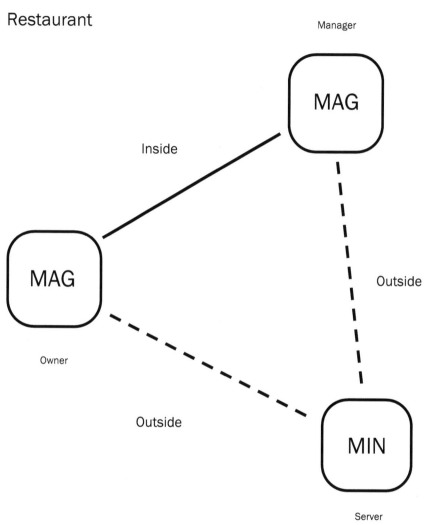

Figure 4.7

Same situation, different triangle. In this triangle the manager is a
Min and so is the server. The manager thinks the owner, a Mag,
pushes him and the staff too hard, resulting in a morale problem
where the staff is not happy in their jobs. When the owner tells the
manager to confront the server, another Min, he does, but
acknowledges to the server that he is glad she gives customers
attention and that the owner needs to understand the importance of
service, putting the owner in the outside position as a Mag (Figure
4.8).

Two Mins/One Mag

Restaurant

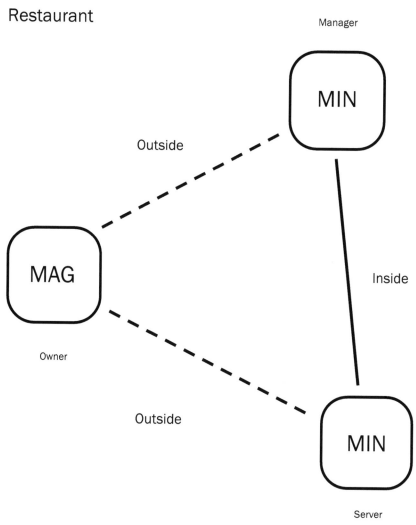

Figure 4.8

If the first triangle, with the server in the outside position, were higher functioning, there would be a productive discussion about how much attention is appropriate for the customers to leave feeling good about their dining experience. If this triangle were lower functioning, the server would become the focus of more and more problems.

In the second triangle, with the owner in the outside position, higher functioning would result in a discussion about morale in the restaurant as the owner hears about the staff needing to take more time with diners and not feel constant pressure to turn tables over. Lower functioning would lead to ongoing complaining about the owner behind his back.

As I said at the beginning of this chapter, the concept of triangles is another way to present the Self in a large and complex context, beyond just the individual person. Triangles expand the perspective from the relationship with another person (dyad) to a three-person system. But it doesn't stop there. Bowen saw the family as a system of interlocking triangles, where a triangle of three people was part of a network in the family of many triangles, all connected in ways that stabilize the whole family. To take it even a step further, in Bowen theory triangles exist across the generations and include people long since dead. For example, an adult woman who idolized her father compares her husband constantly to him and the husband always falls short, as he is in the outside position. This rigid triangle stabilizes their marriage in the present even though the father died 25 years ago.

If one accepts that the Self is involved in this large and complicated network of other selves in patterns that shape who we are, how can a person ever make changes and not be so determined by these forces? This is the power of the Mag/Min framework, now understood as operating in this more complex set of relationships, larger than just one individual interacting in a general sense with the world of other people. This framework is powerful, as it offers ways to be more specific about that person's action based on an understanding of one's own dynamics of Magnification or Minification, and how that works in the network of specific relationships that person lives in.

So how does one change Self in triangles? The change of moving the Home position closer to the Middle on the continuum will challenge and possibly shift the stability of one or more of the triangles the person is involved in. Moving the Home position requires self-focus, first of all to identify the Home position on either the Mag or Min side, but then to understand how one plays out that pattern in relationships with others. In dyads, it is very useful to know if the other person has the same reflex of Mag or Min. A Mag in relationship with another Mag needs to monitor the reactivity of joining with the other and ignoring any limitations. A Mag in relationship with a Min needs to monitor the reactivity of conflicting with the other about limitations. A Min in relationship with another Min needs to monitor the reactivity of joining with the other and ignoring potential. A Min in relationship with a Mag needs to monitor the reactivity of conflicting with the other about potential. This self-focus facilitates neutrality in the triangle.

Thus, the concept of triangles further clarifies how one behaves in the set of three relationships with others who have the same or different reflexes of Mag or Min. In general, change of Self to move the Home position requires self-focus. As one recognizes one's patterns as a Mag or a Min, the person can monitor their reactivity about potential and limitation with others, so that they do not get caught in dysfunctional triangles that stabilize the relationships so that that person ends up always in the inside or outside position by default. With more self-focus, people can behave in ways that allow them to decide to engage another person as they both let the third person be in the outside position because that is what is appropriate for the situation, or decide to stay out of the engagement with the other and be in the outside position because that is what is appropriate for the activity at hand.

A brief example of this self-focused change would be where the Minifier in the outside position of a triangle with two Magnifiers moves from less Minification on the continuum and more toward the Middle, disrupting the stability of that triangle. The outside position based in operating from limitation is now no longer so automatic because sometimes that person aligns with one of the Magnifiers. Or, in that same triangle, if one of the Magnifiers moves toward the Middle by allowing more limitation, it challenges the Minifier in the outside position and the automatic siding of that Magnifier with the other Magnifier.

In the first restaurant example (Figure 4.7) with the owner and manager as Mags, the server as a Min in the outside position could make a change by calmly presenting her position directly to the owner. She could explain that she is providing good service that makes the customers feel engaged in the dining experience and more likely to return and become regulars. This would be a move toward the Middle for her to allow the potential of asserting her position. If the owner agreed to let her continue to take her time with customers and see what happens, this would challenge the old pattern of the owner and manager siding together against her.

In that same triangle, the owner could initiate a change by talking directly with the server, asking her to explain her rationale for serving customers this way in order for him to better understand his business. If it made sense to him and he supported her in taking more time, this would be a move toward the Middle for him by allowing this limitation of having to listen to a point of view he does not agree with, and would challenge the triangle pattern of the manager siding with him against the server.

If the Magnifier in the outside position with two Minifiers (Figure 4.8) moves to a position of less magnification, it disrupts the triangle, because one of the Minifiers has to deal with engaging that Magnifier about potential and not continue to side with the other Minifier in avoiding potential. Or, one of the Mins could engage the Mag directly and leave the other Min in the outside position.

Again in the restaurant example where both manager and server are Minifiers, the Mag owner from the outside position could initiate a talk with his manager, a Min, about how he needs to understand more about what this server is doing that seems so important because he knows he does not understand this need for more time. That would be a move toward the Middle for him and disruptive of the triangle, just as it would be for the server as a Min to initiate talking with the owner and not side with the manager as the other Min complaining about how he does not understand.

Thus far I have described the Self generally and explained how it functions, not as an individual entity, but as an intrinsic part of the dynamics of systems, using the concept of triangles. Because the Self is such an important concept in this Mag/Min framework, as it is the basis for the patterns of decision-making and what changes when those patterns change, I want to define the Self more explicitly. I will do that in the next chapter as I describe the Self as a process of language.

The Self as Narrative

Definition of Self

My definition:

> The Self is a social phenomenon, an entity created and maintained in a complex and coordinated interactive network of humans in which the basis for the interaction is language. It is comprised of two domains: 1.) The brain of each individual, where each person thinks and reacts to their thoughts internally, and 2.) The relationship between the brains of humans as they converse with each other. The two dimensions of the Basic self and the Social self reflect these two domains.

What does this mean? Basically, it means that you cannot know who you are, or be who you are, without other people. They do not need to be present or even alive, but you need the memory of them to have a Self that has a relationship to them. In addition, it means that the way you have a Self with other people is through language. Language here means the spoken word as well as thoughts, because it is not possible to have thoughts without language. (Try to think about something without using ideas, or words.)

Sometimes it is easier to understand something in the negative, that is, what it is not. My definition excludes the notion that the Self is something concrete. Rather, the Self is an idea. It does not exist outside of being able to think about it and talk about it. You can't create a Self from scratch all by yourself. You only have a Self as it comes about in interactions with others and, as the thoughts in your own head are stimulated by talking with others, as you talk with them and they talk with you. This all needs more explanation.

Language

The Self exists only in language. It is created and maintained in language. You cannot think or talk without language. One simple distinction about the difference between animals and humans is that we have language, which allows us to reflect on our experience. Animals can live only in the present. Language allows humans to reflect on the past and to project their experiences into the future.

This is the basis for how the Self exists. We can remember who we are and can predict that the Self will continue into the future. As this process of memory goes on for years, the Self becomes quite stable. A person keeps remembering who they are, over and over again.

However, this circular remembering does not go on inside just one's own head. Other people are a powerful force in this remembering. They keep calling you by your name. As they interact with you in the same ways, they remind you of who you are. There is a powerful predictability in how they remember you, and how they expect you to continue to be who you are. My contention is that you need them to maintain this Self.

But this is only part of how this works. As they remind you of who you are, in your interactions with them as your Self, you remind them of who they are in the same way. Then people are who they are, have a Self, as they interact in relationship with others, and the mode of interaction that creates and maintains the Self for everyone is language.

Much of this interaction happens as people talk with one another, in casual relationships like the one with your regular bus driver, or the neighbor down the street, or more familiar ones like your doctor, or the much older and deeper ones with your family members. This is the external interaction. Of course, another major dimension of your Self is the internal interaction, created all the time in the language within your own head, as you reflect on your experiences all day long, grounded in a basic awareness that it is you who is the source of this reflection.

Take the example of a firefighter. He knows he is a firefighter. It is a major part of his identity, who he is. At work, whether on a fire scene or at the fire station, the constant interaction with his fellow firefighters reinforces this identity. He does not lose this identity when he is home with his children or on vacation. His brain remembers this identity. This seems so obvious, but what maintains the powerful stability of this Self is not so obvious.

I claim that language is the process that creates and maintains this stability. The continual interaction with his buddies, with his colleagues in the other emergency services, like police and ambulance EMTs, and with victims of fires, all reinforce the memory in his brain of this idea that he is a firefighter. Outside of this interaction in language, this idea does not make sense. If I were to say that I am a firefighter when I have never had any experience with that work, it would make no sense. It may be an abstract idea I can imagine, but it is not part of my definition of my Self.

In addition to all this interaction with others that reinforces the patterns in his brain of the idea of becoming a firefighter, when he reflects by himself, he interacts with those memories internally. He does not have to be at the firehouse to "know" he is a firefighter. It is the process of language when he thinks about himself as a firefighter when he is alone.

Humberto Maturana

Mag/Min is my framework for understanding the Self and for working to change and improve its functioning through changing the pattern of decision-making that defines the Self. This framework is based entirely in language. For the understanding and operations of the Self in language, I draw heavily upon the work of Humberto Maturana.

Maturana's theory of Autopoiesis postulates that the primary characteristic of living systems is that they are organized to continually produce themselves (Maturana & Varela, 1972). Along with his colleague, Francisco Varela, Maturana coined this new word "autopoiesis." Capra offers a helpful etymology of the creation of this word (Capra, 1996): "*Auto*, of course, means 'self' and refers to the autonomy of self-organizing systems; and *poiesis*—which shares the same Greek root as the word 'poetry'—means 'making.' So *autopoiesis* means 'self-making.'" (p. 97, emphasis in original).

This simple but very complex idea is that all the processes of living systems function, through ongoing coordination of actions, to keep the organism alive. The organism stays alive only because it is always in a state of producing itself through sophisticated patterns of coordination.

He maintains that this is how all living systems operate, including human beings. However, at the level of the human, he adds another dimension to this process of autopoesis, and that is language. In this theory language is not a vehicle of communication between two separate people. Instead, language is the process of how human beings maintain themselves as human beings. How does this happen?

The coordination process in general for all living systems is a coordination of actions that keep the organism producing itself. They do this constantly by making distinctions of things out of the background. Cells distinguish pathogens in their environment and coordinate actions to respond to the threat in order to stay alive. Animals distinguish predators so they can take action to stay alive. An example I use for humans is of two people walking down the sidewalk toward each other. They each distinguish an object, a person ahead of them, and realize they need to coordinate their actions in order not to collide. We do this all the time, and this conserves each organism so neither is damaged. However, language takes the coordination to a different level. Maturana describes language as the coordination *of the coordination* of actions. What he means is that humans interact and develop abstractions that allow them to coordinate as they make distinctions of their distinctions. In my sidewalk example, the two people would be in language if one calls out to the other and says: "I will move over here and you go over there," and the other replies: "Okay."

This example demonstrates the phenomenon of making distinctions of the other and developing the shared distinction in language about their relative positions in space, but Maturana takes this still further. He says that while an individual person can make the distinction of a Self, separate from the background in coordinating all the various actions of staying alive in the world, they can also make distinctions of those distinctions, and operate in language to create a Self. This is how Maturana understands consciousness, the awareness of one's Self. In their book that presents a summary of this complex theory, *The Tree of Knowledge,* he and Varela say (Maturana & Varela, 1987):

> For our present purposes we wish to explore the key feature of language that radically modifies human behavioral domains and makes possible new phenomena such as reflection and consciousness. This key feature is that language enables those who operate in it to *describe themselves* and their circumstances through the linguistic distinction of linguistic distinctions. (p. 210, emphasis in original)

Basically a person develops an abstraction that is that person's Self. Someone comes into a room and sees an object with a flat top and four legs. As they make that distinction, this object becomes figural.

It stands out from the background of other objects in the room. An animal could presumably see the same object and interact with it by hiding underneath it or jumping on top of it. The human sets a book on top of it. But as the human takes that action, they have the conceptualization of it as a "table." This is a distinction of the original distinction of noticing the object as figural in the first place. And this distinction in language coordinates their action of placing the book on it because that is a well-established and appropriate action that goes with a table. The animal just interacts with it without this additional distinction. But table is an abstraction, an idea for a class of objects that this object fits into. The word "table" spelled out or said aloud has no relationship to these pieces of wood joined together. However, that word coordinates that human's behavior and their behavior with other humans as they too recognize the abstraction of "table." A friend may say, "Go ahead and place the rest of your other books on the table."

It is the same with the Self, but a step further, as the distinction made that is abstract is not about an external object but about oneself. The distinction of one's sense of being figural, standing out in relation to the rest of the world, becomes a Self as one makes a distinction of that distinction using language to create this abstraction of one's Self. Who one is becomes an idea, a class of particular thoughts and behaviors, a personal "category" that defines the person over a lifetime. And it coordinates that person's thoughts and behaviors within their own brain and in interaction with the brains of others.

However, it is critical to understand that one does not make the distinction of one's distinctions as a Self by oneself. Maturana is very clear that this autopoesis of one person's self only happens as that person "couples" with others to create that distinction of distinctions. He says (Maturana & Varela, The tree of knowledge, 1987): "We work out our lives in a mutual linguistic coupling, not because language permits us to reveal ourselves but because we are *constituted* (italics added) in language in a continuous becoming that we bring forth with others." (p. 234)

Maturana's ideas are very complex and challenging, too much so to be explored in this book. (A very useful and understandable summary and interpretation of Maturana's theory can be found in *The Web of Life* (1996) by Fritjof Capra.) What is important for the reader here is to understand how Maturana's theory underlies my Mag/Min framework about the self. This is evident in two ways. 1.) The reader can recognize the essential element from his theory of the coordination of living systems in my conceptualization (based also on Bowen theory) of the Basic self as inextricably coordinated with the Social self, and the Social self as functioning in coordination with the selves of other people. 2.) One can also see the autopoetic process in my conceptualization of the stability of the Self, as it maintains itself in the continual interactions with others in language. In sum, Maturana's theory underscores the fundamental assumption of my Mag/Min framework that it is through language that one changes the Self as one works to change the pattern of decision-making.

Survival and the Self

Another important facet of language and the Self built into my Mag/Min framework is how it functions in the process of denial. As presented earlier, Becker asserts that it is the human's awareness of mortality that creates the existential paradox. The person has a typical body that will die, but can imagine being unique and living forever. This awareness is only possible because of language. It is language that creates the existential paradox, but also provides the necessary protection from the resulting existential anxiety in the form of denial. So language creates the dilemma, as well as the solution, ultimately in the form of the Self. It is language that allows the creation of the Self, which then operates as a denial mechanism. It functions as protection.

Animals have to protect their bodies to survive. They have instinct to enable them to do that. As humans we have evolved to operate in language, which has become part of how we survive. So we have to protect not only our bodies, but the Self as well. We have to protect the denial mechanism that protects us from existential anxiety.

But what is the relationship between the body and the Self? The body is directly connected to the Self of each person because you cannot have a Self without a body. The physical body is certainly not an idea, but it is not the Self either. So what is the relationship?

The answer essentially has to do with the brain. For one thing, the brain can exist only in a body, and a brain is required to do language. While that brain interacts in the world with the environment outside the body and with other brains, it also interacts in myriad complex ways internally with the body in which it resides. It gets to know that body well, as there are highly developed, complex patterns that are coordinated throughout the organism. It also gets to know the patterns of interaction of that body and brain with the world outside that body and brain. Neuroscientists talk about the brain creating maps. These could be understood as a representation to itself of well-established neural patterns. If one focused here on the process of memory, one could then also understand the brain as having a "map" of the Self, which would be a representation of the patterns of coordinated interaction in language within the person and with others as they continually reflect on and remember who they are. This is a very simplistic depiction of the idea of the Self as a map of neural patterns in the brain which fits with my conceptualization of the Self in the Mag/Min framework. The neuroscientist Antonio Damasio has explored this idea of the Self and brain in depth in his book *Self Comes to Mind* (Damasio, 2010).

To have a body that is always at risk of perishing, like the bodies of animals, is worry enough, but to be able to reflect on that vulnerability, which language allows in the process of introspection, is just too much. So we have a Self that enables us to pretend that we will not die. If we had to worry about dying every moment, we would be consumed by that anxiety. Simply stated, having a Self allows us to pretend that we don't have to be on guard constantly and can go about the daily life of a human being. The Self is protection from existential anxiety. This is the way language becomes an important part of survival for the human.

Stability through language

The protection does not come from simply having a Self that can be identified by a person themselves and in interaction with others. It comes from its being stable. Through the ups and downs of daily life and over the course of a lifetime, it remains stable.

This stability can be understood as a set of patterns that happen in the coordination with others and within one's own head, in language. Think of your name. It identifies your Self, but it achieves its stability with a sophisticated coordination of many factors within your brain and those of others who know you. It has a sound that is recognizable, and words that distinguish you from others. If the name is the same as that of others, further distinctions clarify it by family or tribe, by generation, by geography, and so forth, with all of these variables requiring further coordination with others. The further the refinements, the deeper is the validation of the uniqueness of your Self, but it requires more and more interactions with others to achieve this more refined and stable Self.

All of this has you as the central focus of the interactions with others. Now, think of how this is what is happening for everyone else, too. Everyone needs everyone else to maintain their Self as we interact in language, developing more and more stability through well-established patterns.

Much of this coordination happens automatically, like the use of one's name by oneself and others. Another part of this coordination comes about with choices a person makes that fit who they are, the Self, identified by that name. In this way, people recognize that person by the consistency of the decisions they make. Mary would never use drugs. That is just not her. Bob is always generous. People just know him to be that kind of person. These other people also know who they are, as they know their patterns of interacting with that person, which then validates their Self through these patterns. I always say hello to Joe when I see him because he is so friendly. I never talk to Sally because she is so disagreeable. Everyone gains the stability of having a Self, regardless of how positive or negative, functional or dysfunctional, it may be. These patterns can be seen over time by tracking decisions people have made at various points in their life.

Narrative

While the charts in this book provide a very useful way to plot and track decisions over a period of time to gain a sense of the patterns that provide the stability of the Self, stories provide another way to track patterns by using language to incorporate even more information.

One of the essential ways we know who we are is our history, our biography. We organize the memories of our life into stories. And of course other people are an essential part of our story, as we are of theirs. So the narrative of our individual life and that of our network, be it family, country, tribe, or culture, is fundamental to the stability of the Self, as language functions in this way to provide coordination and balance for all the relationships. Changing the pattern of decision-making, which of course is the focus of this whole book, then changes the Self in the network of its relationships, because that changes the narrative for that person and for others in relationship with that person. It certainly can be disruptive as anxiety emerges, but as the story is disrupted, a new "chapter" of the story can be created, which then creates a different balance in the set of relationships.

Usefulness of the narrative mode

Stories are very basic to human interactions. Today neuroscientists, with their major focus on memory, think that stories may provide a way to organize memory, as a person can incorporate many details too difficult to remember as a list, into a sequence of events. Daniel Siegel, a neuroscientist, describes narrative well in his book *The Developing Mind* (Siegel, 1999):

> This connection between interpersonal and individual process is clearly seen in an important aspect of memory, the narrative telling of our life stories. . . .The telling of stories has a central place in human cultures throughout the world and plays a crucial role in the interaction between adult and child. From an early stage in development, children begin to narrate their lives—to tell the sequence of events and internal experiences of their daily existence. What is so special about stories? Why are we as a species so consumed by the process of telling and listening to stories?
>
> By the second year of life, children begin to develop the "later" form of memory, called declarative or explicit, which includes both semantic (factual) and episodic (remembering oneself in an episode in time) memory. "Narrative" memory is a term referring to the way in which we may store and then recall experienced events in story form. "Co-construction of narrative" is a fundamental process, studied across cultures by anthropologists, in which families join together in the telling of stories of daily life. (p. 60)

So how can this idea of narrative help a person understand the larger context of their patterns of operating from Magnification or Minification, and use it in working to change the Self through decision-making?

Basically, narrative can provide a way to organize the many complex factors that comprise the Self as a stable entity, one that we recognize with such regular familiarity as "just me," so that one can see the patterns of that stability and then track changes in the Self. Narrative is also a way to understand the coordination of the Basic and Social selves. While the Basic self is primary, the Social self is essential, as it provides a way for people to interact with others in managing the anxiety about their existence. Our biography, our story, is a way to grasp both the Basic and Social self as who we are as *one* Self, both as we think about ourselves by ourselves and as we interact with others.

Again, it is important to emphasize how stable the Self is. People notice when there is a major change in Self, like an alcoholic who gets sober, or a mother who becomes depressed, but people just presume stability otherwise. What could be argued is that the stability is what is remarkable, not the lack of it, given all the complex systems that interact with such coordination.

The Mag/Min framework, based in systems theory, accounts for this stability of the Self as a phenomenon that emerges out of the balancing of many systems. One of those systems, as has been presented, is the neurological one which makes language possible. As stated above, one person's brain is part of the family system or social system of the other brains that interact and develop a large and complex balance.

This chapter presents the idea that narrative, both an individual's biography and the story of that person's family or culture, provides a way to understand the stability of the Self as part of the balance of these complex and interacting systems. It is this stability that allows one to track changes in the Self. The rest of the chapter presents examples of narratives from three domains that depict different patterns, followed by a section on what change in those narratives could look like. In this way the reader can see how language and narrative form an essential component of the foundation for this

Mag/Min framework.

Note that throughout this book and specifically in this next section on narrative, the locus of change is always the Basic self. The process of change is one of self-focus to identify the patterns of reactivity, either magnifying or minifying and then to act differently. As one does this over time, the interactional patterns with others, the Social self, will change. A person can use the awareness of the patterns of the Social self, whether they are the same as the primary (MAG/mag or MIN/min) or different (MAG/min or MIN/mag), to complement the work with the Basic self, but not to make the fundamental changes that move the Home position closer to the Middle on the continuum.

Narrative domains

Individual patterns

The first phase of understanding one's own narrative is to put one's individual behavioral patterns of either magnification or minification into the story of one's life. Once you have identified your Home position as Mag or Min, can you look at your history and see the many ways this pattern is demonstrated?

If you operate from the Minification side, can you see the ways you have limited yourself over the course of your life, perhaps since adolescence? Maybe you were shy and afraid of other boys or girls as a teenager. As you got older, you may have let others propose the next steps in your life, like marriage or a career. You may well still let others go first in many ways, to the point of asking your children too much for help.

If you are a Magnifier, can you see the ways you have over functioned through the course of your life, perhaps since adolescence? Perhaps you were the gregarious one as a teenager, always the extrovert, a leader. That may well be how you got married and divorced. Perhaps you are very successful now in your job, but very busy and driven to succeed even more. Or you may be elderly and fighting the aging process with lots of vitamins and exercise.

Figure 5.1 depicts examples of decision tracks for four different people starting out from the same Home position, with blanks provided for you to fill in with various topics, like parenting, occupation, finances, health, religion, and so forth, that may have shaped significant decisions you have made over the course of your life.

Profiles

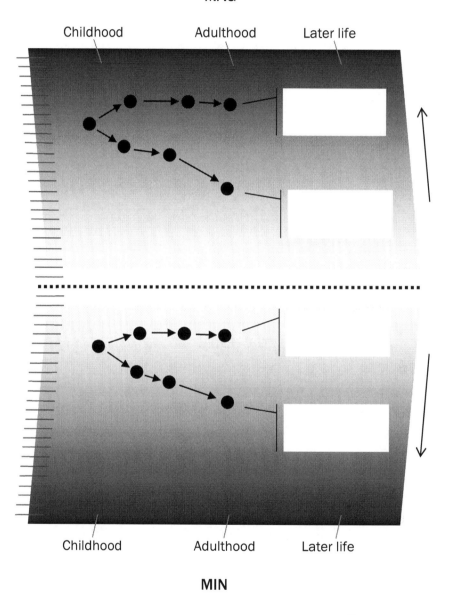

Figure 5.1

Relationship patterns

Everything discussed to this point is your individual narrative, understood as a lifelong pattern of magnification or minification. But that is just you. Systems thinking is about how your individual pattern never stands on its own as a pattern. It is always part of a larger pattern that maintains it. So the second phase is to consider your relationships with others and them with each other in terms of Mag and Min.

The Minifier who has let others take the initiative for her life may well have come from a family with a strong work ethic, parents who worked hard to accomplish goals of succeeding financially and providing for their children. In the face of these go-getters, she may well have taken a more passive stance about social relationships, academics, and then marriage and having children herself, where these children have become assertive like their grandparents. So her pattern of minification plays an important part in this family's overall story of striving for success, where she has always been the focus of concern from both generations, by her parents in the previous one, and her children in the next, as not being quite good enough as a daughter and as a mother. This pattern maintains her minifying.

Now the Magnifier. This person comes from a similar striving family, but her role has always been to participate in this constant attempt to meet goals and succeed, whether it is initially to have a boyfriend, or later a husband, who is attractive and successful. If she marries a husband who also operates from the Magnification side, then they are very active and assertive in their jobs and with their children as parents. Their daughter, who has always been passive and struggled with failure, becomes a major concern for both of them, but probably has more of a conflictual relationship with her mother, who is worried about her ability to make it as a woman in the world if she is too passive.

Whole-system patterns

The third phase is to think of the overall narrative of the larger family or organization itself. Here one can think in terms of ethnic and historical patterns, as well as family patterns over many generations.

While being careful not to lose systems thinking and fall into a reductionist stereotyping of a whole people or family, it is possible to distinguish themes that people in those ethnic groups or families would easily recognize and see as an important part of their identity.

The Irish are well known for their melancholy, for the history of oppression by England. One could think of that in terms of a theme of minification. It is also possible to think of Blacks in the United States with a history of slavery as a theme carried on through racism as one of minification. One might think of Germany, with its character as being organized and efficient, as one of magnification.

It is critical to assert at this point, that simply being part of an ethnic story of either magnification or minification in no way determines whether an individual person or family has a Home position that is the same. While the individual's denial mode, may be affected by that larger narrative, it is also possible that this larger ethnic or historical narrative is not as powerful a determinant of one's Home position as the story of one's own particular family.

A family that has a congenital history of a debilitating disease like muscular dystrophy may affect the individual narrative of a person four generations down from the person who first manifested the symptoms. A Minifier in this generation decides unequivocally not to have children. A Magnifier, assuming the muscular dystrophy is "ancient history" and too far away to affect him, has children without any concern for genetic inheritance.

Or, take a person coming from a family with a great-great-grandfather who made a fortunate financial investment in the railroads in the 1800s in the United States, who could end up dealing with great wealth passed down through the generations. Then the question might be how that has affected how she has lived her life always one-down to the success of her parents and grandparents, never feeling entitled, always feeling she owes people, a Minifier. By contrast, the Magnifier would always feel entitled and expect to succeed more than others who are seen as "not trying hard enough."

One can also think of the narrative of an organization. A person who begins with a novel idea and develops a product in his garage, which he then starts to produce in larger quantities and sells to a lot of people, may feel like a rebel in the face of the established businesses in that field. His product is better, but he is the underdog. Eventually, as he grows the business and becomes an established force in the field, his vision of that organization, as dominant and established as it has become, may still be that of the rebel, the underdog, as he continues to experiment in his R & D department with contrarian ideas that seek to challenge others. While very successful, there is always a sense of working from one-down, never quite entitled to embrace success and accept his standing as a powerful leader in the field. This is an organization that operates from the Minification side, and that ethos pervades the organization.

From the other side would be the company that began in the same way, but with an assumption of competing against the major businesses with the goal of being the dominant company in the field, to the point of always scanning the market to make sure no one gets ahead of them. This would be an organization that operates from the Magnification side.

Change across all systems

Now think about change. This is the fourth domain. How does changing one's Home position of Magnification or Minification from farther out on the continuum to a point closer to the Middle, as elaborated in Chapter 3, affect one's individual story and the larger narrative of one's family or other social system? Take any of the examples listed above.

What happens as the shy, teen-aged Minifier described earlier, who went on to allow others to make important life decisions for him, takes an initiative in his marriage to challenge his wife about her career, because he now wants more of a life partner as he considers retirement when she has no intention of retiring? How does that change his sense of himself as an individual, and how does that change the story of their marriage, considered as successful by each of them and by their families, now in a situation in which this happy nuclear family may break up?

Or what happens to the lifelong extrovert, described earlier as a gregarious teenager, who has lived a life driven by the need to succeed, but now decides to stop fighting old age, be quieter, and accept the limits of being older? How does she see herself now? Is this a story of ultimate failure, giving up after a life of success? Or is it a story of finally slowing down enough to embrace life to have a peaceful ending? And how does that play for her family? Are her two children, who operate from the Magnification side, disappointed at seeing their mother giving up and now worried about their own futures? Does her husband, who has always operated from the Minification side in this marriage, where he always went one-down to her initiative, feel the challenge of matching her change of being calmer and more present by no longer deferring and having to be more present to her, as she is more emotionally available as she gets ready to die?

How about the two from the families that strive for success? What if the Minifier decides to pursue some goals for herself, like going back to school for a professional degree? How do her mother and daughter treat her when she graduates and is no longer so "inadequate"? Or what if the Magnifier decides to stop trying so hard to get her daughter to be more assertive and accepts her own role as a more supportive mother, rather than a "successful" one? How does her daughter accept this different mothering, and does her husband see her as being a less responsible parent and partner?

Or how about the magnifying Irishman, who allows himself to deal with the melancholy in his own life as he finds himself in an unhappy marriage, and has to sort through his lifelong fight with his heritage to always have an optimistic outlook, even if it took alcohol to maintain it? How about the Black woman who has always fought for her rights and the rights of her people, who at some point acknowledges how hard she has fought against the impact of slavery without realizing how this has alienated her from her daughter, who early on developed a pattern of minification.

Or the German laborer who has always been a leader, now a union organizer, who realizes his fight with bosses has been about his own struggle never to allow anyone to dominate, and relates this to his German ancestry? What happens as he decides not to run for union president and deals with the disappointment of his fellow workers?

Or the Minifier with the history of muscular dystrophy who decides to use genetic counseling and reconsider having children? How does this change his identity as a possible parent and his relationship with his wife? Or the Magnifier from that family who becomes more concerned about genetics and decides to talk with his children about their having children? Or the Minifier from the wealthy railroad family who now fights for her inheritance with the intention of improving her life for herself and her nuclear family? Or does the Magnifer who has always felt entitled to the wealth passed down through the generations of his family decide to begin to make substantial donations to charity and become a philanthropist?

Or either of the CEOs from the businesses of minification and magnification? What if the minifying one decides to soften the contrarian edge and revise the business model to be more powerful by competing as the forthright dominant company, instead of as the pseudo upstart? How would that change the way his employees see their work? What if the magnifying CEO decides to modify the business model to have less of hard-edge competitiveness, and that changes the company's view of its place in the communities where it is located? How would that change how the employees view their working for this company now?

These changes across all of these domains are all changes in the narratives that change the Selves of these people, and affect their relationships with others they interact with.

Narrative as a tool

It is useful to distinguish the general process of language as a coordination of brain function, from the more specific language process of narrative, which is the focus of this chapter. In the previous chapter, I presented the concept of triangles, and then framed it in terms of the general process of language coordination. How people talk and think from Mag or Min is part of how the triangles balance, whether it keeps the person in the inside or the outside position. Language can be used to change one's position in a triangle, for example, by not always defaulting to words and thoughts of minification, and thereby not maintaining the balance of consistently being in the outside position with two other Mags. Or a Magnifier can speak and think in ways that acknowledge the reality of limits and change their automatic position of the inside position with another Magnifier.

While language can be used over the long term to change patterns, it is different from language as a story. Narrative is a sequence of language events that flows from one to the other in ways that make sense of the overall sequence. In the Mag/Min framework, language as narrative is also a tool, but on a larger scale than each specific decision and action that is a part of a larger pattern. Narrative allows one to grasp the larger pattern as a whole. In that way one can use that broader perspective to make specific decisions from a greater depth of understanding of one's Mag or Min pattern.

There are three ways narrative can be used as a tool in this Mag/Min framework: 1.) To identify the Home position initially; 2.) To track changes one makes over time; and 3.) To keep working with those changes to make more changes.

Along with the ways presented in Chapter 2 to identify whether one operates from the Magnification or Minification side of the continuum, narrative provides an additional one. People can reflect on the decisions they have made over the course of their lifetime and often recognize a pattern of either magnifying or minifying. As a person reflects on how they have lived their life, they may realize that at many turns in many different realms they have opted to take major risks in the expectation of achieving more. It is not just a pattern, but a sequence of decisions that tell the story of their life. That story helps them identify their Home position on the Magnification side. The same is true for the person whose biography is one of always worrying about not making it and playing it safe that helps them identify their Home position on the Minification side.

The second use of narrative is to track changes. If the Magnifier has made some decisions that reflect a change in the pattern, where he has accepted the reality of some limitations, he can see that change over time as a shift in the storyline of his life. He may remember a particularly difficult and important decision, like leaving a marriage or a job, and see how his life changed as he became less driven when he began to think differently when confronted with limitations. Or a Minifier may know that she has worked hard and made changes in her Self by trusting her own judgment, relying less on the approval of others, and see in her narrative how that change is apparent in a variety of different realms where she has made decisions that have made her more powerful.

The third use of narrative is as a tool to work with changes already made. As a person reflects on the story of their life, that person can now use that narrative, including the changes, to monitor Self to further modify the pattern of magnification or minification to move even more toward the Middle. The shifts evident in the story to date serve as a baseline for future changes.

For example, a man from the Minification side who makes changes to allow for more risks, and succeeds in achieving some important goals with those decisions, can identify where they happened in the timeline and what they led to. Then, when confronted with another difficult decision about taking a risk, and feeling a pull to default to the old pattern of minification, he would be both supported and challenged by awareness of his story. If he reflects on his previous experience, he cannot talk himself into limiting assumptions that it really won't work out or that he is not really capable. The evidence is there in his own lived experience. It does not come from someone else telling him what to do. While challenging, this realization can also be supportive, as it allows the anxiety that comes with taking a risk, knowing he has done it before and it has been productive.

Of course, the tool works in the same way for the person from the Magnification side who looks back on her story and sees how much her decisions to stop and not take an unreasonable risk have prevented the old pattern of burnout and actually produced successful outcomes, in spite of not trying so hard. That narrative can be useful as she confronts decisions about "opportunities" that she knows she should reject, as it is both challenging and supportive.

It should be easy to grasp how the patterns of magnification and minification play in the various segments presented above. The reader may simply understand them as inspiring human stories, but I want to underscore the underlying theoretical perspective of the language coordination in the brains of people who make up these social systems. This is important, because as one hears about these individual people making changes in their lives, and gets a sense of the power of those changes from the stories, I want the reader to understand that power in terms of language and the brain. These narrative snapshots of change reflect more than people overcoming particular problems. They display the outcome of work over the long term of understanding patterns, and experimenting to change the coordination in one's own brain as one interacts with other brains, *in language*. Then the impact of reading these narratives is in recognizing them as a series of examples of an effective and practical way of living life more fully. And now the next chapter presents more complete stories that demonstrate this long term work.

Chapter 6

The Stories

My Story

First, my story. I will tell it as a sequence of important events in my life, through decision points that can be tracked as part of lifelong patterns. This provides the reader with a concrete example of the dynamics of language in the coordination process with my family system as I present my narrative.

Now, beginning with Figure 6.1, I have included additional specificity in the standard longitudinal chart to portray the systemic dynamics that underlie the decision-making process for a person. You will notice that the difference between the lighter Middle and the shaded extremes is defined as a force of pulling up or down. The system tends to pull the person back toward the old stabilizing patterns of decision-making, either Magnification or Minification, and it requires effort to do the work to resist that pull and move the Home position up toward the Middle. Plotting the decision-making patterns over time now can be seen in terms of the person's managing the self and the pull of the systemic forces.

Systemic

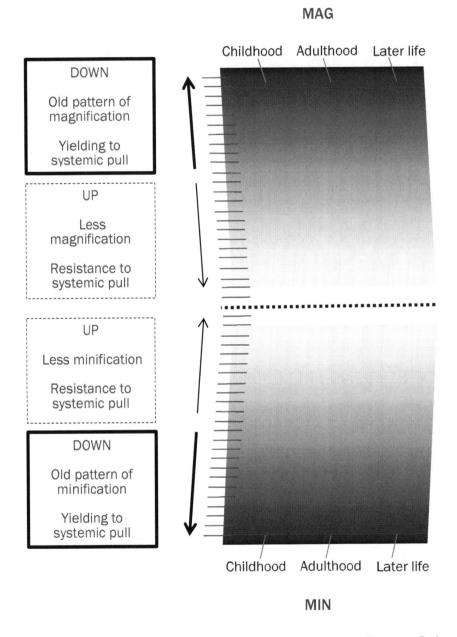

Figure 6.1

This chart is a template for the tracking charts that follow. They display the content of the specific decisions and the background of the systemic issues that are the context for those decisions.

Figure 6.2 presents the content of my narrative in a graphic form. It displays the trajectory of my decision-making patterns: where they maintained the status quo; where they demonstrated regression to older and less functional behaviors; and where they indicated growth and change. For me as a Minifier, growth is movement toward the center of the continuum, upward on this longitudinal chart, away from the regression of more limitation. Decisions in the shaded boxes above the midline indicate either maintenance of the status quo or regression to a lower level of functioning. The three clear boxes represent seminal decisions that moved the Home position more toward the Middle and a higher level of functioning. Use the chart as an outline to follow the chronology of the narrative of my autobiography, but also use it to track my changes in the pattern of minifying decisions which are embedded in the dynamics of the system of my family.

My story will be followed by two composite stories, one from the Magnification side and one from the Minification side. These are additional examples of the concept of the self as narrative in the context of the dynamics of the systems these people live in. These examples are constructed out of the real-life stories of my clients.

My Decision Track
Through the Life Cycle

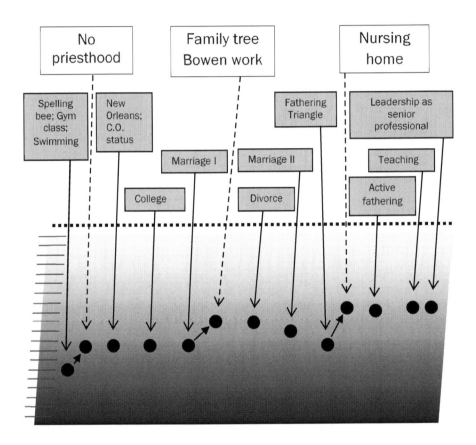

Figure 6.2

Lifecycle stages

Childhood/Adolescence

Elementary school

I was born in Rochester, New York and lived there for all of my childhood and adolescence. I was raised as a Catholic and went through Catholic schools from kindergarten through college. As an only child, I remember my mother walking me to school for the first day of kindergarten and my being terrified when she left me outside in the school gathering area with all these strange kids, except one neighbor girl to whom I stayed glued that day. My mother walked away and did not look back, which I realized later was a surprising strength on her part, given how my relationship with her played out with school attendance over the coming years. My mother was always taking me to the doctor for sore throats that I was not sure I had. I would have to stay home from school if there was even a slight possibility of being sick. I remember swallowing hard many times in the morning when I woke up to see if I was really sick or not. There was a sense of relief, but also guilt and confusion, when I could feel a little soreness and did not go to school.

This struggle continued for most of elementary school, but on balance I did not miss a lot of days and did well academically. Nonetheless, I was very shy and always tried not to stand out, which was made more difficult because of my high grades. I did well in spelling bees in my classes and was once selected to compete for a scholarship for high school. I was up on stage and did okay, but made a mistake near the end, disappointing my teacher, who knew I could have done better and maybe won.

One time I was playing in my neighborhood and a kid from across the street got mad at me and hit me. I had never been in a fight before. I was shocked, and hurt, not physically but emotionally. I ran home and my mother comforted me. One of my uncles happened to be visiting and he told me to go and hit the kid back. My mother dismissed that idea immediately and I was relieved. Minification.

Surviving and doing well through elementary school could be understood as functioning adequately with my mag Social self (MIN/mag), even with my shyness. The Min Basic self can be seen in my yielding to my mother's concerns that I might be sick and needed to stay home from school, and in the likely sabotage of my success in the spelling bee that I think my teacher recognized. I was certainly not aware of all of this anxiety as a child, except to know that I was afraid of standing out in any area.

In a recreational gym class, I dreaded counting off by numbers and ending up first in line of that subgroup. One time I saw my father tell a lifeguard to make me jump into the water and do an exercise he knew I was capable of, because I was staying back and not moving forward to do it. My father took me to the pool many times throughout my childhood, and I went on to become a good swimmer. He also taught me the game of golf, which I was good at but always sabotaged my good play under pressure. I continue both of these sports to this day in my 60s, but I trust my abilities in both of them now more than I did when I was younger.

Overall, there were no major choices to this point, just responding and coping with the Basic self of minification, and the Social one of magnification.

High school and college

I went on to a Jesuit high school that had an entrance exam and high standards. I got in and again did well academically, even though I did not think I was particularly smart. For the first three years I remained shy, taking the bus across town, doing my school work, returning home by myself to do my homework, and going back again the next day. At home, I remember being very lonely and at times depressed about what life had to offer in the future. During these years, my mother became depressed and saw a psychiatrist regularly. She had ECT (shock therapy) several times, but despite some periodic improvements, she never really felt better.

While I did run track and cross country from freshman year on, it felt more like an individual sport than being part of a team. However, my life changed some, as I did become more involved in social activities in my senior year, becoming a member of the cheerleading squad at this all-boys high school.

I did not have attendance struggles in high school, but my hyper-vigilant anxiety about my health continued. Several times, while playing golf with my father, we would stop and he would take me to the doctor for an EKG because of my concern about chest pains, but the tests never showed any indication of heart problems. Once my doctor took me into his office, alone without my mother or father, and asked me something to the effect of why wasn't I living my own life as a teenager. Did I realize I really was not sick? I remember being completely confused about what he was talking about. These chest pains were the same as the sore throats in elementary school.

My first choice point occurred when I decided not to enter the priesthood from high school. In a conversation I initiated about my future because I had to decide about college, my senior-year homeroom teacher, a Jesuit I liked a lot and trusted, told me he was certain I did not have a "vocation" and that I would be fine going on in the secular world. I felt guilty but relieved, and decided to go on to college and not the seminary. This was similar to what my doctor had been trying to tell me about living my own life, but I still did not understand the dynamics of my relationship with my mother and my family. I did however begin to understand something about trusting my own experience in the talk with my homeroom teacher, because I did not think I really wanted to be a priest. Deciding to become a priest would have been out of duty, a debt to be paid, similar to the duty to make my parents happy. This shift also fit trusting my experience of my body in not really being sick throughout childhood and adolescence. Actively rejecting the priesthood was a move toward the Middle, a change from the previous level of minification.

This event appears in the first box of the top row of the chart, which is not shaded because it reflects a significant move toward the Middle.

Young Adulthood

College/Social movements

I applied to Catholic colleges and chose a Jesuit one about 90 miles from my hometown, in Syracuse, New York. I knew I was choosing to get away from my parents. It worked very well, as I was too far away to come home regularly, but close enough to return home when I needed to.

As the Jesuits challenged me to think and question, I became involved in the civil rights movement in the 1960s, and went to New Orleans with a Catholic organization one summer to live and work in one of the projects in the city. I took liberal stands against the hierarchy of the Church, especially about the Latin mass, and supported the ecumenical movement to collaborate with other religions that the establishment opposed. I increasingly became against the war in Vietnam and obtained Conscientious Objector status. However, these strong stands were other-focused, not grounded in my Basic self. They helped to define me socially, as I was engaged with others in college and community groups, but inside I did not feel strong. This was my mag Social self. When I was knocking on doors to hand out antiwar and civil rights leaflets, I was always hoping no one was home.

Along with this operating from a Basic self of minification were deeper feelings of anger and depression. The anger was toward my parents and "the Establishment," whether that was the Catholic Church, the government, university administrations, whatever. The depression led to feelings of being very lonely, especially during the summers when I returned home from college. My mother had gone back to work when I went to high school, and my father played a lot of golf, leaving her a "golf widow." They did not have a strong connection with each other and I felt very alone. During these college years, I was still maintaining the same level of minifying, as I was choosing to avoid being powerful and strong with my parents by not saying "no" to responsibilities to make their lives happier, and not saying "no" to being part of their marriage in the triangle with my mother in the inside position, and my father in the outside position (Figure 6.2).

This deeper loneliness with a lower level of functioning of Basic self continued in spite of the social relationships at college that my Social self of secondary magnification facilitated.

Upon graduation from college, I chose to marry my girlfriend from college and live in Syracuse. This was another min-maintaining choice, as it functioned to keep me from returning to my home with my parents. In addition, my pattern in that marriage was to yield Self and not assert myself. Still, no significant moves outside of the narrow range of minification on the continuum through age 22.

Career Part I

My career went well from the beginning. Over the next 15 years or so I went back to school and became a social worker and a marriage and family therapist, and eventually a supervisor of other therapists in both fields. I worked in a public mental health agency for children and families, and opened a private practice, which I still maintain over 40 years later. I carried over the Social self of magnification in my work, as I became a very good therapist, and especially as I challenged the status quo of the establishment in the mental health field. I became a systems therapist, going against the prevailing model of psychoanalysis, a non-systems individual theory, promulgated by the psychiatrists who were the bosses in the mental health facilities. Despite this progression in my career, the effort was other-focused, not movement toward the Middle based on strength.

Family work from Bowen theory

As mentioned in the Preface, some movement began to happen when I learned about Bowen theory and started to do the required genealogy work. Bowen *therapy* operates out of Bowen *theory*, which Murray Bowen developed in the 1960s through to his death in 1990. It is a theory about how humans function and is grounded in how systems in nature operate. As explained earlier in Chapter 3 regarding changing the Home position, one of the major concepts is the differentiation of Self of a person in their family, similar to the differentiation process of cells in living systems. Here I will present the differentiation process in more detail as I describe the work with my family before I had discovered Mag/Min.

The fundamental variable determining the maturity or level of functioning of a person is the ability to distinguish feeling and thinking. Automatic reactions, based in feelings without much consideration of the dynamics of a relationship, and what the consequences of one's actions will be, is considered "reactive" and lower functioning. More thoughtful, considered responses to feelings is higher functioning, a more differentiated response. For example, a knee-jerk response to blame one's partner for being late again before understanding the situation, is reactive. Taking the time to understand the circumstances, and then respond, is higher functioning.

However, it is critical to understand that Bowen theory is a systems theory. That means that a person's functioning, or level of differentiation of Self, becomes a pattern of responses that is inextricably part of the dynamics that balance the system of their family. The Self, who you are and your patterns of operating in your family, is largely determined by the patterns in your family. For example, a person may have the personality of a rebel in her family. She always takes an oppositional point of view. Bowen theory would consider this a reactive pattern, as her responses are primarily feeling-based, but would also understand that this is a predictable pattern that organizes the responses of others, as well as hers, in the family. Other people come to expect her opposition and they develop predictable responses to her opposition. There may be the sibling who always argues with her and the parent who always tries to placate her. This is simply a pattern in her nuclear family.

Taking this understanding further, Bowen theory views family patterns through a wide lens, extending back through many generations of a family, exploring the family history of people long since dead. For Bowen theory, this is the operational view of the family, a multi-generational system. The work involves constructing a "genogram," which includes the information typically in a family tree, but with much more information. A genealogy focuses on the lineage of a family, who is descended from whom, whereas the genogram includes information on the wider family of aunts, uncles, cousins, and so forth, to understand the patterns across the larger family, not just the pedigree of descendants.

Running counter to all this determinism are the theory's assertion, and the experience over the years of many people using this theory, that it is possible to change, to raise one's level of differentiation. The hallmark method of this work of change is to return to one's family of origin and experiment with acting differently from the old and predictable pattern, with more differentiated responses, in dealing with the actual people in your family, especially those in previous generations, namely parents, grandparents, great-grandparents, aunts, uncles, and so on.

This is what I did in the 1970s. My mentor during those years was a family therapist who had met my parents in a demonstration family therapy session I volunteered for as part of my therapy training. She asked me afterward if I realized how hurt my father was that I did not know his family. I had had no idea. It was the same experience of my doctor telling me as a teenager that I was deeply fused with my mother. That was the beginning of several years of doing my family work. I went to visit family I had never met before, and many relatives I never knew I had in the first place. That created anxiety, but it did not stop me from setting up visits and asking questions. I was trusting myself, using the structure of Bowen theory to engage people and be strong in simply presenting myself and asking questions.

There were times when my shyness and anxiety about initiating contact, especially when I knew enough about the family history to understand some of the conflicts, made me hesitate. This was minification. However, the momentum of the work carried me along to keep making phone calls and visits, drawing genograms, and entering the data in a family tree computer program. Over these years, I came to be seen as the family history expert. Then they began contacting me, both to obtain information and to offer new data. I eagerly went to family reunions. Some of the competence and respect I felt still came from my mag Social self, but the move to engage my father's family in the first place came from Basic self and was a move toward the center of the continuum.

I did this genogram work on both sides of my family. It gave me a way to understand my loneliness and depression in the context of the pain and loss in both my mother and father's families over the generations. I could now understand the source of my feelings of hopelessness as my not being able to make my parents happier, especially in their marriage, which had failed to compensate them for their losses in their childhoods.

Here is a brief summary of that history of my parents' emotional deprivation in childhood. The losses on my mother's side were the deaths of her siblings before she, the youngest, was born. Her oldest brother died at age 21 in World War I just after enlisting in the Marines. Her two older sisters had died within the same week from diphtheria in an epidemic in Rochester in 1911. This blow was compounded by the death of her mother's mother in Ireland, the same year my mother was born. My mother's mother had not seen her mother since she emigrated from Ireland many years earlier.

Then my mother's next older brother became a serious alcoholic, creating a great deal of stress in the family. My mother's mother did not have a lot to give my mother, given how much her grief had depleted her.

On my father's side, his mother died when he was two years old. His father remarried and that wife became pregnant, but died in the hospital of a drug mistake and never came home with her baby. His father remarried a third time, and that stepmother was said to be unkind to the children, not providing a loving environment. So, both of my parents came out of their childhoods with a lack of nurturing from their mothers.

Beyond the important benefit of understanding my family's past, the genogram work also became a way for me to define myself differently going forward in the triangle with my mother and father. As I got to know my father's side in much more depth, I became less aligned with my mother and her family. This was freeing and eventually led to my divorcing my wife, since the primary function of that marriage, to keep me from my family, was no longer needed. These two changes, engaging my family of origin and divorcing my wife, combined to move me more toward the Middle on the continuum. As a result, I began to feel much more connected to my family, and not so angry and depressed. (But the impact of the Bowen work had only just begun, as will be evident in later decisions.) On the chart this period is marked in the non-shaded box in the top row, reflecting the move toward the Middle.

Middle adulthood

Remarriage

After a year or two of being single and dating, I remarried. This too was not a move toward the Middle, because I wanted to be married again and this seemed like a good relationship. As time went on, I struggled as I questioned whether this was a good marriage, but this time my Bowen work kept me grounded in an effort to stay self-focused as I tried to understand my struggle in terms of my patterns from my family of origin. That definitely helped, but a few years later I went along with the decision to have children, when I did not feel like I wanted them, which again was based in minification and not a decision that came from a position closer to the Middle.

Being a father

In the beginning, being a father was another experience of making decisions from minification, as I had a very hard time setting limits for my children. I was the good guy who left a lot of the necessary, tough stands to my wife, establishing that position in our nuclear family by getting angry with her for being so "hard" on them." As time went on, I knew I was in a weak position by always working to align with my boys to be the understanding father, often in opposition to my wife. This was not a deliberate mode of decision-making but rather one that became a strong pattern, as I kept finding myself responding in the same reactive ways.

Over those years of their childhood, I made efforts to take stronger stands with my children, but it did not become a major undertaking until my oldest was a teenager and my youngest was in elementary school. The next developmental stage of my parents' moving into later life, described below, gave this fathering project much deeper grounding, as I was able to operate less from minification from that point on.

Nursing home

Both of my parents were Minifiers. My father was a machinist, a very good one, but always saw himself as lower in social networks outside of his own socioeconomic status. He was intelligent but never went beyond elementary school. My mother was a very nervous woman. She too was intelligent, and did finish high school, going on to what was called "Normal School" for teacher-training. She dropped out quickly because the children made her too nervous. She became thoroughly involved in raising me, which I have described above, and can be understood as aligning with me in the inside position in the triangle, with my father in the outside position.

When I went to high school, my mother went to work as a secretary. Even then I realized people liked her, but began to struggle with being concerned about her anxiety and having to take care of her. Her minifying was apparent (MIN/min), but my father's was not, as his Social self was mag, because he over functioned in the marital dynamic with my mother's under functioning. As I learned more about Bowen theory and our family history and patterns, I became aware of his neediness and his Basic self of minification that was masked by his over functioning as a secondary mag (Min/mag).

Both of my parents loved me deeply and were very active in their parenting. They worked hard to provide for me, to pay for a good education, including college, even though they did not understand higher education or what I was studying. However, my leaving home was a crisis for them, as my mother had yielded Self too much in the effort to cope, and my father did not know how to relate to her now as a husband not as a co-parent.

They both retired and maintained a stable relationship, with my father spending a lot of time golfing and visiting with his family. My mother stayed home but went to her sister's regularly. My mother never learned to drive, so my father took her there often, sometimes every day. My father kept trying to engage their marriage, but my mother remained depressed. They stayed involved with my father's family and with my mother's two sisters and niece. Later, they spent winters in Florida for quite a few years, with my father golfing and my mother going along.

As they aged, they became less able to take care of themselves. I was still living 90 miles away. I knew I could not have them come and live with me, and they did not want to leave their home. I visited as often as I could, managing my own ambivalence about feeling a duty to help them as well as maintaining my parenting and work responsibilities. I hired home aides to come in and cook and clean for them. My extended family also helped them, with one of my cousins in particular taking on the task of watching over them, the aides, and their finances. The situation reached a crisis point when the director of the home aide agency said she could no longer take responsibility for the care of my parents in their own home.

Neither of them was sick or debilitated, mentally (dementia) or physically (ambulatory). My mother continued to under function, not taking care of basic hygiene, and my father was helpless to engage her. She was still depressed and began to cut herself off from many people, including my children, her only grandchildren, finally refusing to visit or even talk to her sister, who had been her lifelong support. My father struggled to keep the marriage alive, but was frustrated. This was more of the same for them, operating from minification and maintaining that pattern in the face of this crisis of the life-stage change to later life. Others felt sorry for them and tried to help, but then would be puzzled and sometimes frustrated with not understanding why they could not function better given their clear strengths. These people did not have a way to understand the situation. While I did not have the explicit Mag/Min framework, I did know my parents were functioning at a relatively low level of differentiation. I also knew that I had caved in to this pattern for many years, yielding a great deal of Self in alternating between trying to help, getting frustrated, then angry, then distancing, and then coming back again for more, all the while feeling responsible for them and their happiness.

I responded to this crisis of their being unable to be cared for in their home any longer with a decision that changed my life from that point on. For once I did not default to minification by trying to convince them to take better care of themselves, or by letting others take over and take on responsibility for their care like a family member, an eldercare agency, or the Department of Social Services. Instead, I told my parents that they needed to make efforts to take better care of themselves, not relying on others completely to do what they were capable of doing, and if they did not, I had no choice but to place my mother in a nursing home.

My mother begged me not to do it, but simply ignored the question of doing more for herself. It was very challenging for me, but I held my position in the face of her tearful protests in our living room in the home where I had grown up. I proceeded to make the arrangements to place her in a nursing home, which I did several weeks later. Instead of taking over in anger, I was able for the first time in my life to see my responsibility to take charge of her physical needs, but not try to manage her emotional needs by trying to make her happy. She protested vigorously, but from the one-down position of a victim refusing to address anything she herself could do to change, and, except for her 50th wedding anniversary party in the nursing home, remained mute until she died. She never talked to me again. While placing her in the nursing home was a major step for me, I still allowed my cousin to actually take her there, a slip back to some minification.

My father remained at home, but was lost without my mother. Soon after her placement, the same nursing home had an opening and was willing to take my father. So he went there too. They were in different units, with her in a skilled nursing unit requiring a higher level of care, but they saw each other daily. They had the marital separation I think my mother had wanted all along.

One of the most powerful emotional experiences in my life came at the time I drove my father to the nursing home. I realized that my parents would no longer return to the home I had grown up in. I left him at the nursing home and drove back to that house, crying all the way. When I got back to the house, I decided to go into each and every room and allow the memories of childhood to emerge. I cried deeply, sobbing for a couple of hours. I knew then that this was the right thing to do.

What I did not realize right away was how powerful an experience my initiative to place them actually was. For once I did not default to minification in this life-stage crisis. I began to realize, as time went on, visiting them in the nursing home, that I felt much freer, not angry and depressed. I could let myself love them in a way that was not possible before. This was in spite of the fact that my mother's cutoff intensified, as she had become mute by choice. I visited her in the nursing home every few weeks but she refused to speak to me at all. I deliberately maintained contact in our "conversations" that were essentially monologues on my part. This became an important connection for me with my family, as the relationship had changed significantly for me from reactive anger and depression to openness, sadness, and acceptance.

While my parents' deaths a few years after entering the nursing home were certainly painful and significant as life-stage changes for me, they were not at all the predictable emotional disruptions they could have been had I not made the changes in my patterns of minification. I was able to be calm and powerful as I delivered the eulogies at each of their funerals.

Over these years, I began to better understand the patterns of my minification and the larger multigenerational family patterns, especially around pain and loss. I realized that I could now distinguish that, as my parents' only child, I was responsible for their care and safety, but not their happiness. I could not overcome the suffering from each of their families in previous generations, as described earlier. This understanding and my move toward the Middle on the continuum leveraged powerful changes in other areas of my life. Again this event is depicted in the third, non-shaded box of the top row on the chart.

My nuclear family

As a parent the effort I had begun of asserting more limits with my children now had a much clearer foundation with this new understanding of my responsibility for my own parents. I was responsible for many things for my children as a parent, but not their happiness. This freed me up to set the limits my children needed and to share the parenting responsibility with my wife. As a son, I also recognized that I was not responsible for my parents in the same way I was as a father for my children. From some of my clients' work I knew that treating aging parents like children reflects a confusion in the generational boundaries, making it difficult to parent one's own children. So in my own situation, not being responsible for my parents' happiness freed me to be their son, and to be appropriately responsible for my children as a father. My continued efforts to take stronger positions have resulted in a better relationship with my children.

Career Part II

By now my career was progressing very well. My private practice was full, and was a major source of income. Many of my clients were therapists themselves, and so I had become a therapist's therapist. Therapists also came to me for supervision. This supervision work also included part-time work at Syracuse University in the Marriage and Family Therapy program, training graduate students.

Later I was invited to teach at Syracuse University in the School of Social Work as an adjunct faculty member. This eventually led to teaching the equivalent of a full-time load as a part-time faculty member, still maintaining my practice, but at a reduced level.

Clearly I had become a leader in my field. But this is trouble for a Minifier. The anxiety created by my successes pushed me to discount them. I would deflect compliments from my clients about what a good therapist I was. Similarly I would tell supervisees that they knew as much as I did. I would be surprised when my students would want to know more about what I thought, rather than about what the authors of the readings had said. I could also see the confusion and frustration of all these people, clients, supervisees, and students, when I would put myself down in the face of clear evidence of my competence and leadership. They did not understand what was going on, and then were not sure about how to handle me because they had a sense that it was not humility but something else.

I gradually began to recognize that it was actually anxiety, the same anxiety of allowing a move toward the Middle that I had felt in deciding not to become a priest, to be stronger as a father, and to place my parents in a nursing home. So first of all, I worked deliberately to simply not discount compliments. Then, not having undermined myself and subsequently having to recover ground already given away, I was better able to stand firmly in front of my classes and in my practice with my clients and supervisees and be strong with my ideas. This was my Social self becoming more congruent with my Basic self as the Home position shifted closer to the Middle. They were still distinct but less opposite.

This effort was also reflected in my writing. It began with my work in supervision, when I realized that my way of supervising was different and powerful, as my supervisees and colleagues recognized. So I wrote an article on "my" model of supervision, which was published in a juried professional journal. When I realized that many students, supervisees, and clients liked my ideas and wanted to stay in touch with me, I decided to establish a website for my ideas. I have maintained it ever since, self-publishing essays as my ideas emerge. Finally, you have in your hands the culmination to date of my efforts to make a move toward the Middle through my writing.

Later adulthood

Retirement?
I write this book now from this lifespan stage of later life. I am realizing that to retire at this point would be minification, because I have reached a point in my career as senior person in my field as a professor, therapist, and writer that I need to remain powerful and

make my contribution. An element of this decision clearly involves dealing with my old pattern of being an only child, so that my decisions now need to be taking initiative to engage others in larger networks of communities as a leader. It is minifying to operate as an only child and stay more separate as I age.

Golf?

One might think that golf fits in this section on retirement as a stereotype of a man who retires to play golf every day, but that is not how it fits here for me. As I have described earlier, golf was an important part of my father's life. He taught me the game and I have played it all my life. What I have not said to this point is that I have played it always as a Minifier. My wife can testify to how often I would come home discouraged after playing. I can remember losing matches constantly as a teenager to a friend, probably a Magnifier, always assuming I would eventually lose even when I was hitting better shots than he was. And I always did lose, sabotaging myself when I was playing well, just as when I lost in the spelling bee in elementary school. That pattern continued through all of my adult years playing the game, until the last several years. Since my changes described above in moving my Home position closer to the Middle, I am much better able to accept the ups and downs of good and bad rounds, tolerating the anxiety of doing well. But it is still a challenge at times.

Systemic understanding

It is very important to understand this story in terms of my family as a system. I tell it as my story, and the charts so far track only my decisions, but it takes some effort to see my changes happening within the ongoing dynamics of my family system, and not distort the perspective into seeing me as an individual person making autonomous decisions. As explained in the previous chapter on the Self as a narrative, which describes the stability of the person and the stability of the family of Selves, I will now put my story into the context of my family, and show how their patterns maintained their own stability, as well as mine. My changes are shifts in my participation in the ongoing stabilizing patterns of my family. On the next chart (Figure 6.3) I have added the factors that have been present all through my life and have been the deeper context of larger patterns in which I have made my decisions.

The three shaded boxes at the bottom represent larger issues in my family system that were important factors that influenced me in my decision-making, as they pulled me back to my more automatic pattern of Minification. The four clear boxes at the top identify the powerful "rules" or assumptions I no longer accepted which made my changes in the patterns of decision-making possible. They explain the pull up toward less Minification while the shaded boxes at the bottom explain the pull down to more Minification. These systemic factors, both up and down, will be described below.

Systemic Context of Decisions

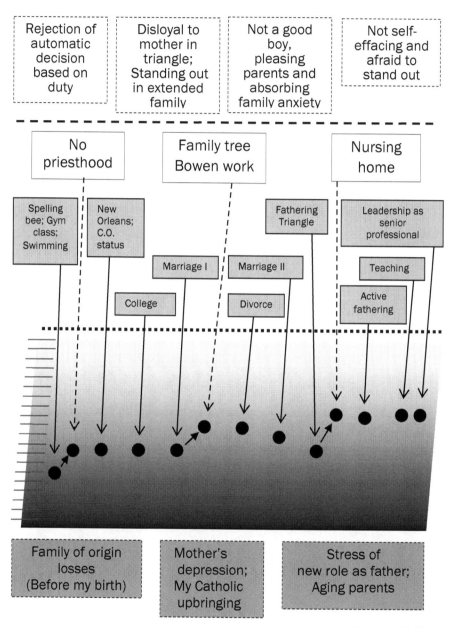

Figure 6.3

My mother, my father, and me

In the triangle with my mother and father, I was in the inside position with my mother for much of my life, leaving my father in the outside position as he struggled to have a satisfying marriage, given my mother's over-involvement with me throughout my childhood. Her depression when I left home kept him in the outside position. My inside position played out in my hyper-vigilance about my health; in my reactive anger about her holding onto me; and in our constant involvement with her family. See Figure 6.4.

Parental Triangle

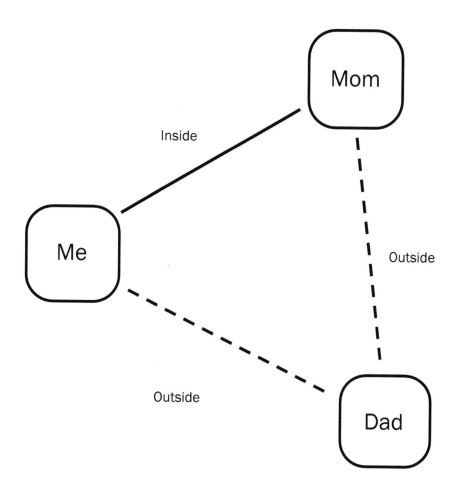

Figure 6.4

My minification was part of the stabilizing force to maintain the triangle in my nuclear family. I was afraid to take positions that would threaten my parents, as I began to feel a primary responsibility for both of them from a young age. With the shift in the triangle with my parents, as I did the Bowen work, I began to feel closer to my father. But almost simultaneous with that was the legitimacy I felt of my anger toward my mother. Previously, from my Catholic upbringing, the anger was wrong, a sin, which led to depression and more minification. Gradually I became more able to disagree with my mother, let her know when I was angry, and not yield Self with distorted apologies or depression of my own. I experienced this shift as freedom from the limiting dynamics of depression and minification that were based in assumptions of responsibility for their happiness. This responsibility played out in ways I did not understand until adolescence.

Later I understood more explicitly how responsible I felt for my parents, and became aware of my fears of threatening them. I was very afraid of disappointing them, of hurting their feelings. I remember my father praising me for being such a "good boy" because he never had to scold me. At the same time, I was afraid of my anger, assuming it was a sin. My Social self was being "a good boy," an expression my family often used to describe me.

This Basic self, operating from the Minification side, was a powerful force in maintaining my over-involvement with my mother and under-involvement with my father. It also helped to maintain the long-standing distance in their marriage, as well as my mother's intense closeness with her family and my father's being outside that family, seen as the "insensitive" husband: a blue-collar worker who was not sophisticated enough.

The fact that both of my parents were Minifiers was also a major factor in maintaining our triangle. My father did not feel entitled to challenge my mother about her relationship with me, or about her over-involvement with her family. He got mad about it, but would never take any stands in regard to it. My mother was afraid of everything, especially about offending people. She desperately did not want people to be angry with her. The irony was that her passivity and refusal to take responsibility for herself resulted in others first trying to take care of her, and then getting angry with her when she refused their help to improve her life, maintaining her minification of under functioning.

My extended family

I also began to understand the larger forces in the family that helped to maintain the stability of me and my parents in our nuclear family triangle. My distance from my father's family manifested the larger, interlocking triangles of my father and his family together as one leg in the outside position, with my mother and me as the other leg in the inside position with her family. The reader can see this triangle in Figure 6.5, which depicts the level of systems larger than just individuals.

Larger Family Triangle

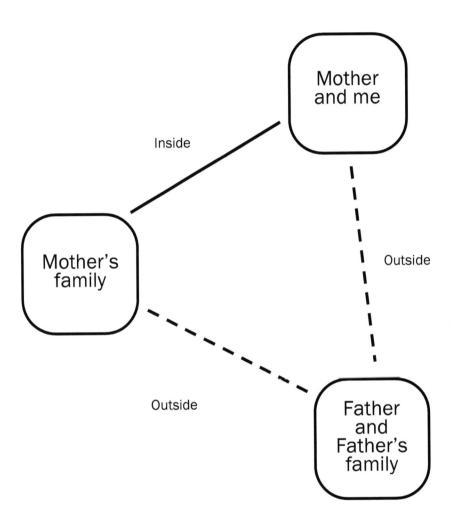

Figure 6.5

Doing my mother's genogram helped me understand the patterns on her side of the family. As described earlier, I discovered how many serious losses through death there were on her side, which explained her fears and her operating from the Minification side in this family, where she did not want to make things worse by asserting herself and her needs. That perspective helped me to not regress and give up my changes, as I could allow myself the legitimacy of my anger about how her under functioning affected me, but not try to change her. I became better at accepting her as I began to understand her pain and the pain in this family. I began to allow myself to love her and told her so later in the nursing home, even as she remained resolutely mute.

From exploration of my father's family, I learned about the major losses in his nuclear family as described earlier. With the deaths of my father's biological mother and his first stepmother, and the additional stress of the conflictual relationship with his second stepmother, it makes sense that he grew up not feeling entitled to being a strong person able to take charge of his life. As a Minifier he married my mother, another Minifier, and they produced one child, me, who ended up supporting their stabilizing mechanism of coping with these painful losses through a pattern of minification in not threatening them, but instead acting "responsibly" from my Social self.

While not going into the specific patterns of other people, like my aunts, uncles, and cousins in both my mother's and father's families, I want to point out that these patterns of magnification and minification operate in the same way to maintain the stability of their individual selves and their nuclear families. In addition, each of their nuclear families participates in the maintenance of the stability of all the individuals and of the larger extended family itself. This is the comprehensive perspective of systems theory and systems thinking. It is how I understand the specific forces I have dealt with in my family, as I have made my changes to shift my Home position and thereby disrupt my participation in those multiple stabilizing patterns.

There is one other way to look at the stabilizing dynamics of the family at the higher level of multiple generations that affect individual members, and that is ethnicity. The differences in the ethnic roots of each of my parent's families further supported my minification and my position in the triangle on the inside position with my mother.

It is important to note here that the following specific analysis of my family may seem to be based on stereotypes of ethnic cultures. It is useful to distinguish between recognizing possible characteristics that go together to describe familiar and commonly occurring phenomena, from a reductionist assumption that portrays the description as true for the whole culture or everyone in it. Rather, the characterization can be a general description that can provide a powerful explanation for similar patterns for different people, not accounted for in other ways, while acknowledging that the general description will not fit everyone or fit for all time.

My mother's family is Irish and my father's is German. One could generally characterize the Irish culture as oriented toward minification and the German toward magnification. The Irish culture is prone to melancholy and to feeling one-down. Ireland has a long history of being oppressed, which helps to explain this orientation of minification. The German culture values pragmatism and efficiency. They do not want to be dragged down by feelings. They prefer the one-up position.

These stereotypical differences played out in concrete ways in my family. My mother always assumed a one-down position, and her sister, who was aligned with her and very supportive, was always very understanding of my mother's fragility and protected her. An important dimension of my aunt's understanding was how "sensitive" my mother was. My aunt was a staunch Irish woman, steeped in the Irish culture, and she had an ongoing conflict with my father about his being "insensitive" and not understanding of his wife's struggles in life, which my aunt attributed to his German heritage. My father would get angry with her for putting him down, but also dismayed at her sentimentality, which fostered her impracticality and carelessness about finances, as she would go deep into debt, spending irrationally, an Irish Magnifier.

Both of these negative characterizations by my aunt based on cultural identifications were distortions, because my mother was under functioning, capable of more strength than she would allow (minification) and my father was a highly sensitive person, easily hurt. But the point is that these two cultures, Irish as Minifiers and Germans as Magnifiers, played a part in maintaining the triangle with my parents and myself as I sided with the sensitive, Irish side by being very involved with my mother's family and having much less contact with my father's practical family.

Summary of systemic processes and dynamics

In Figures 6.2 and 6.3 the reader can see the track of these major decision points over the course of my life to this point. As I see it, the major changes in the automatic pattern of minification occurred at the three seminal decision points identified in the clear boxes on the chart: 1.) The decision not to become a priest; 2.) The decision to do the Bowen work to engage my family differently and redefine my position in the triangle with my mother and father; and 3.) The decision to place my parents in the nursing home.

The "rules" for me that contributed to maintaining the balance of my family system, and stabilized my Self in it, could be characterized by the injunctions to: "Be a good boy, obedient"; "Do not offend or upset others"; and "Do not stand out." The outcome for me of following these rules was my depression, anger, and self-sabotage. The top row of four boxes presents this context of my violating those system-stabilizing rules over the course of my changes.

These two figures demonstrate the idea that the system is always in motion, seeking the stability of an overall balance, and that decision-making is a part of that process, either yielding to the old patterns, or making changes that change the balance of the system.

Since this has been the presentation of my story as a Minifier, the chart necessarily represents only that side of the continuum. So I have included a blank chart for Magnifiers (Figure 6.6) to see graphically the opposite pattern in which UP (actually down on the page toward the Middle) still represents a shift away from the old pattern and DOWN (up on the page) a yielding to the old pattern.

Systemic – Mag Track

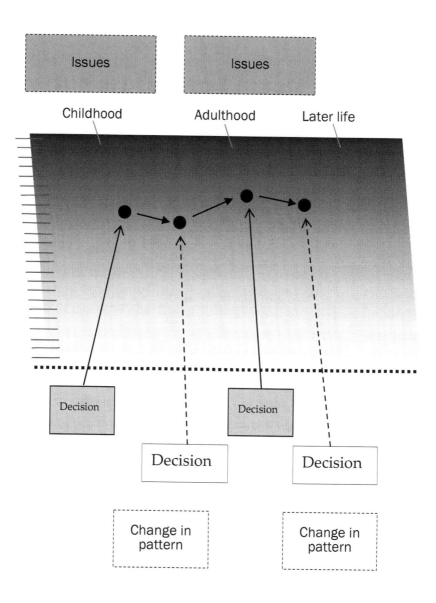

Figure 6.6

To grasp the complexity of all the systemic interactions that make for the ongoing stabilizing balance of my family system, try to imagine this chart of Decision Tracks for *each* person in my family, so that I am the context for each of them and each of them for each other! There is no chart that could possibly diagram all of those patterns of interactions, but the individual one of myself that I have presented here at least offers one perspective, one dimension, which depicts my part in contributing to the dynamics of my family system by the patterns of my decision-making.

My changes over the long term—Momentum

When one considers the change process of an individual as I have presented it here in my story, and put that process into a systemic framework as I have just done about my family, there is another important element that emerges and needs to be understood. That is the dynamic of momentum. As I have said throughout the book, systems are always in motion. That is how they maintain stability. If a person changes their pattern, disrupts the system, and maintains those changes over a period time, the system will adapt to create a different balance. But that new balance is not a static point. The system continues to be in motion.

The resulting experience for the person making changes is momentum. They feel both a pull to move forward with these new behaviors, as well as a discomfort with acting and thinking in the old ways. Their changes carry them along and challenge them to change more. They are not in control of their own changes.

These decisions and the actions that followed changed my participation in the patterns of interaction in my family. I yielded less to minifying, which clearly disrupted the stability of my relationship with my mother and changed my ability to have access to my father's family. The momentum of these shifts in the Home position closer to the Middle clearly changed my relationships with my children. It was not until I placed my parents in the nursing home, making a major move toward the Middle on the continuum, that I began to change as a father and co-parent with my wife. One could say that as I found my role with my parents as a son, not as a pseudo parent for them, I could more clearly distinguish my role as an actual parent of my children. Then the change toward less minification from the nursing home placement enabled me to change my parenting of my own children to be less from the Minification side. Had I continued to operate at the same level of functioning, at the previous level of minification, I most likely would have maintained the stability of the old pattern of trying to be a good-guy father, dragging them into my marriage, as I was continually critical of my wife for being too mean.

Along with these changes in my family relationships, my professional life also changed. I had always known I was a good therapist. My clients told me so and I could recognize my good work in the clear changes they had made in their lives. My practice has thrived over the years and many colleagues and clients have told me about my excellent reputation in the community. I also have known about my competence from the large number of people who have sought me out over the years to work with me as a supervisor of their clinical practices. However, what has changed with the shift of my Home position is my taking on more responsibility as a therapist, supervisor, and teacher now with the identity of a senior person and leader in the field. I began to accept this competence, instead of discounting it with pseudo modesty.

This all demonstrates the continual momentum of the work on Self. Once the changes begin, as the person makes the changes in the pattern of decision-making to move more toward the Middle, the momentum of the changes does not stop. One change leads to another. For the Minifier, new events come up that challenge the person to continue to maintain the stance of not defaulting to decisions that block the possibility of favorable outcomes. But each successive success prompts the person to not only do it again, but to do it at a higher level of functioning, prompting further movement of the Home position toward the Middle. But this means more anxiety and more vulnerability, and more success, and on and on.

So there is pressure from the momentum to continue to take more risks and allow more potential from the change in the Basic self, but there is also pressure in the social realm. As I find myself more able and successful in my decision-making, I am able to act that way in social interactions with more ease. There is more congruence as I am stronger in interactions with others, and they recognize it and begin to trust my acting with less minifying reactivity. Then, as they trust me more, it presses me to trust myself more, which accelerates the momentum. If my Social self were min, and not opposite, the change in the Basic self would challenge the Social self to not minify as much. It would match the shift in the Basic self.

For me now, monitoring my minification not only allows me to maintain the gains of self-acceptance described above, but also allows me to give more. The difference is that as I am more powerful with moving toward the Middle, I am stronger and more confident about what I have to pass on to others, and I will take more risks to make a contribution. In the past, with more minification, I would have assessed the probability of a favorable outcome as not as likely because I had discounted the value of what I had to offer. So I am powerful *and* *humble* as I am part of a generational process that is much bigger than me.

The momentum continues for Magnifiers as well. For them new events challenge them to continually decide to accept limits, which leads to their being more powerful also, but not in the old way of asserting their strengths, but in accepting what they cannot do. Then the challenges increase with their successes as well, along with the anxiety and vulnerability, as they are powerful in accepting limitation, moving toward the Middle from the other side of the continuum.

In sum, had I not made these changes in the pattern of minifying decisions, I would probably have maintained my self-sabotaging career choices. Whenever my successes as a therapist or teacher emerged, I would have continued to discount them in the old way, disrupting the good work of my clients and students. My writing would probably never have gotten done, because it would never have been good enough, and this book would never have been published.

Instead, these decisions have resulted in a change in my patterns of decision-making, which has led to a higher level of functioning in my behavior and in my relationships, which is shown in the charts of my Decision Track as a stabilization of my Home position closer to the Middle than it was in my childhood.

That is my story and my changes. Now I want to tell two other stories, one of a Mag and one of a Min. These two people are not actual people but composites of real people, clients I have worked with. Rather than present actual client material, I have chosen to combine the problems, family dynamics, and work in therapy of several people who represent each pattern of Mag and Min. In this way I protect the confidentiality of my clients. In another way it offers a more universal portrayal of the two denial modes because the composites draw from various family patterns, genders, occupations, and problems, enabling different readers to identify with specific parts of the pattern of Mag or Min in this "person." Like my story, these two composites give the reader real-life examples of change over the long term.

Other Stories

MAG/mag—A father

Don was a college professor, and a good one. He always worked very hard, preparing at great lengths during the summer before courses began in the fall, and then was constantly searching for more material to include when he was in the middle of teaching the course. He was very dedicated to his students, always encouraging them and offering to help them to make sure they understood, always having a hard time giving them a fair but low grade, assuming that their failure was somehow his failure.

After years of this, he crashed. His own son was having serious emotional problems. He and his wife had been separated for a year and his son was living with his mother. However, his son spent half the week and every other weekend with him. Don had been very involved in his son's education, just like that of his students. He spent a lot of this time with his son helping him with schoolwork, because his son had a learning disability. But now he was failing his sophomore year in high school. Of course his father re-doubled his efforts to tutor his son, to the point of neglecting some of the responsibilities of his job at the college. He would be late for his own classes and miss deadlines for turning in his grades. E-mails from his disgruntled students began to pile up in his inbox.

His son began to withdraw from him, saying he did not really care about school anyway. Don and his wife had been separated for a few years and now they began to have more fights about his intensity in pushing his son too hard. He realized he was getting depressed. He felt out of options and did not know what to do.

He had come from a family in which his father was generally passive and his mother was in charge, though she was unpredictable, and could get very angry if people crossed her, especially if she was drinking. Don was the oldest in the family, responsible for his younger brother. Don was smart and capable. He always did well in school and was well liked. He knew how to get things done and often helped his parents, as well as looking out for his brother. His father appreciated his son's managing his wife for him. Don knew how to help his mother extricate herself from conflicts with neighbors and her own family. Many people did not know she was an alcoholic.

Don could never understand people who procrastinated or were incompetent. He had no patience with them. But now he was becoming one of them, and this terrified him.

He came to me desperate for help, wanting to know what he could do to get control of his life again and solve all of these problems. He had never sought help before because this was the first time he had not been able to meet a challenge by just pushing his way through it with hard work and determination, ignoring all the costs. We began with my telling him that his old way of dealing with a situation like this could not work. He simply had to give up on trying harder. He had to figure out what he needed to accept as a limitation, something he could not overcome.

This in itself was a major challenge, but not one he expected from a therapist in the first session. Still, enough of the rationale for it made sense and he trusted me, so he was willing to explore this counter-intuitive idea.

He started working on changing his behavior with his son by controlling his strong impulse to help his son with his homework. When his son would come home from school frustrated and upset, Don worked very hard to not immediately ask him what the trouble was and press to help him. This was extremely difficult for Don. He felt very bad for his son, and bad for himself that he was being a poor father for not offering help he knew he could provide, even though it probably would not be helpful. His son's grades continued to slide, and periodically Don would make a mistake and offer help, which his son generally rejected. Sometimes they would try together again, but it never really worked. His son felt bad about his schoolwork and Don felt bad too, but the tension in their relationship was diminishing.

Don got calls from his son's teachers asking for his help because they were used to his strong support, and now were disappointed with his new attitude. This made Don feel even worse. Don's wife also became concerned about their son's schoolwork, but she had to admit that the father-son relationship was less tense and that she and her husband were fighting less. Despite all of the anxiety and the pain of feeling unable to help his son who was having a hard time, Don began to trust himself and what he was doing. In some way he knew it made sense. While it was confusing, he began to feel stronger as a father as he let himself be appropriately helpless.

He then experimented with this new perspective with his own students. In classes he followed the students' particular interest in parts of what he was presenting that day, and let go of his agenda of having to cover everything he had planned. He was stunned at how well his classes went, as his students got very interested in the material, asking very good questions and seeming to understand without his trying so hard to get them to understand.

His son failed his sophomore year, which was very painful for him. Instead of yielding to the old pattern by setting up a new, intensive study program, he took some clear, self-based positions with his son. Rather than absorb his son's anxiety and make that failure his own, he challenged his son to come up with ways to improve his academic performance.

At first the son resisted, simply withdrawing and saying he would just drop out of school. Don was clear with his son that he would not allow that. He also presented some options and some consequences for what his son decided. He suggested his son meet with each of his teachers and find out what they thought would be an appropriate plan for next year. He might ask them to help him find a tutor. He might talk with his guidance counselor for help. If he did not take action, he would lose privileges like television and video games, have an earlier curfew, and have an increased number of chores around the house.

Don's wife worried about whether he was being too harsh with their son, especially when he complained to her about his father being unreasonable. She told her husband she did not agree with what he was doing, but did not try to stop him. Don was calm, but clear and strong with her that this was what he needed to do to be a father to his son.

It took a while, but his son eventually talked with teachers and the guidance counselor and they worked out some plans for him to get help and improve his academic performance. Over the next school year there were a lot of ups and downs. His son would be surprised and pleased when he got excited about a school project and got a good grade, and then upset and down when he could not understand and did poorly in another subject. Don continued to stay strong, not jumping in to help, but feeling upset and confused himself at points. He also had to enforce some of the limits of no TV and video games when his son was with him. This led to some intense stand-offs, that eventually eased.

Over the course of that year, Don and his son had some good times. He felt closer to his son than he had before. His son acknowledged he hated his father for being so hard on him, but grudgingly admitted he probably needed it and appreciated his father for doing it. In school he did much better, passing all of his classes except English, which had always been the most difficult for him. He then worked with the school to develop a plan to improve his performance so he could graduate from high school. Don and his wife finalized their divorce. She still was not pleased about her husband's change with their son, but did not interfere in that relationship, and their son felt comfortable going back and forth between them.

At work his boss gradually realized how good his teaching was and kept asking him to take on more teaching and administrative responsibilities with other departments in his college, and later with other universities. He accepted many of these projects, but always had the question in the back of his head about needing to be very careful about knowing where the limitation was, just like he did with his son about helping too much. If he could not find something to say "no" about, he knew he was in trouble. He did not like having to be careful about going too far and taking on too much, because he felt so vulnerable about not going all the way, but he was smart enough now to know that that led to more satisfying outcomes.

As a result, he was more productive at work, as he became more selective about which projects he would take on and which he would decline. He began to be more respected by other teachers and administrators as a leader, based on his vision about the school and its mission.

MIN/min — A wife

Sally was a manager in a retail clothing store. The business had been in her family for many years and she had worked there since she was a kid. She liked the work, because she liked clothes and she knew the business well. Her father had started the business and it had always been profitable, but only marginally, because he would get angry and alienate customers and suppliers. Still it survived, in spite of him. Her father had recently retired and now she basically ran the store.

She was married to a lawyer who had had a gambling problem He no longer gambled, but many years of struggling with this problem had taken its toll. He had been married three times, with children from two of the marriages. He and Sally had no children. She married him because she felt a connection with the hard life of ups and downs. He would win periodically but was never able to pay off his debts and ruined his relationships with his children and his wives. Now that he had done some difficult but productive work on himself to manage this problem, she thought she could help him to maintain his self-improvement and build a successful life together.

Sally had no children of her own, but never felt like she really wanted to be a mother. Her relationships with her stepchildren were not particularly strong, as her focus was much more on her marriage. Her husband worked at repairing his relationships with his children, but did not try to get her to be a mother to them. He saw this as more of his project.

Children were not trouble for them. The problem was that they fought as a couple all the time, and it was always about his spending time and money on betting in one form or another. While he no longer got caught up in serious debt, as in the past from casino games, he did like to play poker with a group of friends most Friday nights. He would also buy lottery tickets weekly. She worried this would lead to a collapse into his old problem, though it never really did. She felt like she could never really trust him or their relationship completely, and kept trying to get him to stop.

In her family, she felt like she always did what she had to. She knew that the clothing store made enough money for the family to survive, but she also knew that her father's temper threatened the business at various points and that she sometimes had to take charge. Customers liked the store and trusted her, which made the business viable. However, she would have loud arguments with her father over his behavior. She was always trying to get him to see the error of his ways, but he would never listen. She never felt like he understood her, and she never stopped trying to get him to.

As a teenager, she had a boyfriend who came from a wealthy family. She adored him and was pleased that he liked her better than her girlfriends. After a year of going together, he dumped her for a girl from another wealthy family, more acceptable to his parents, and married her. Sally never really got over it. In her mind this was the ideal mate, and she measured subsequent boyfriends against this standard, never really thinking she would ever be lucky enough to find such a man again. Her current husband certainly validated that assumption.

They came to me together for marital therapy. Her complaint was that he needed to stop betting because it was ruining their marriage. His was that she needed to get off his back and if she was that dissatisfied she should just leave. Early on in the therapy my suggestion to her was to stop trying to get him to change because it is always hopeless to try to get someone to change. This was upsetting to her and confusing to him. She thought this meant that she should give up because the marriage was over, and he was annoyed because he thought the problem was her and he could change if he needed to.

She began the work by focusing more on keeping herself calm by not getting caught going after him when he announced plans to go out with the guys. It would tear her up inside to know he was spending money and risking a slide into his old destructive problem of gambling, but she worked hard to tolerate those feelings without arguing with him about it. At first she felt like she was worse off than before. He got to do what he wanted to do anyway, and she had to be the one who lost, now becoming even more concerned about the marriage. He initially felt relief because she was finally off his back. As time went on she got better at controlling herself in not yielding to the anxiety about him and could get calmer. This did not mean that he did not know that she did not like what he was doing. She would let him know at various points that she did not think it was a good idea for him to spend his money this way; that she did not feel close to him; and that she continued to have questions about the viability of their marriage. The difference was that she did not get into an argument with him, trying to get him to agree with her. This was a huge change. She would state her position and then stop, sometimes repeating her "no," and sometimes just calmly walking away.

Over time, she realized she was doing better. She did not necessarily feel closer to her husband, but she felt much stronger about herself in the relationship and much calmer generally. At work she found herself acting more like a boss, not overbearing, but one who expected more from her employees. She began to feel more responsible for the success of the business, instead of just trying to make sure it did not go under. Some of the workers resented her change, not liking being held more accountable than before, especially compared to when her father was in charge. They knew if he got upset he would get over it and forget about whatever had bothered him. With her now, she stayed much more consistent with her expectations. Some left and she hired some new people that understood the need for productivity in a successful business.

Nevertheless, she continually discounted her changes and this success. She attributed the improvements in the business to everything but herself, like her father's retirement, employee turnover, a better economy, and so on. When employees and other business owners would compliment her and ask for her advice, she would think they really did not know how inadequate she was. She knew she was afraid to trust any of this success because she knew it could not last. To let herself feel competent would set her up to have to deal with "reality" when things turned south, as she knew they would. Besides, she was still not happy, since her marriage was not any more secure than when she began to make these changes in herself.

Gradually her husband began to feel a little nervous about his marriage. He recognized her changes at home and with her business. He worried a little that maybe she did not really love him anymore, because she did not seem to care about his financial situation. He had not slipped into debt, but he suspected his betting had become more of a habit, not something he enjoyed as much as before. In addition, his law practice was not doing that well. Actually her business was doing better now than his, and she seemed to get a lot more satisfaction from it than she ever had before. He knew he felt some relief when she would say that it was not really that successful, but he also knew she was stronger and that maybe she would not need him eventually.

He had dropped out of the couples therapy after a few sessions, but she continued individually for a year, coming every two or three weeks. Now he wanted to resume sessions. He came a few times by himself, but then asked her to come as a couple again, which she agreed to. She was reluctant to commit herself to working on the marriage at this point, fearing she would be settling for a husband who fell so far short of her ideal. At the same time, she was torn because she felt, in spite of all her changes and the successes in business, and feeling stronger and calmer, she did not deserve any better than this. That made her very sad.

So now, the challenge for her in the therapy with her husband was to maintain her strength by trusting herself and considering the possibility that her husband was responding to her change in being more powerful. Just as she felt vulnerable acknowledging success in her business because she left herself open to failing, she now had to deal with the vulnerability of not yielding to the weak position of trying to get her husband to change in order not to lose the marriage. She had to tolerate that loss as a possibility if he chose not to continue.

This was all very troubling to her, but she knew she could not go backwards and give up her changes. It was utterly impossible. So she had to go on tolerating the anxiety and the vulnerability, as she kept on doing what she had been, letting her husband know where she stood about his betting, not trying at all to change him, and acting as the responsible boss at work. She simply had to wait to see what her husband would do.

He chose to continue therapy, but wanted to do it in couple sessions. His general approach was to figure out what he could do to please his wife and then do it. However, when she held her ground about her disagreements with him and he realized he could not find a way to please her, he would get angry and begin to fight with her, which was the old pattern. The difference now was that she was much better able to not get caught in that trap by arguing back with him. She stayed self-focused, simply stating where she agreed and where she disagreed.

After he would get mad, he would have to apologize, again hoping to please her. This just kept him caught. So I challenged him to stop trying to please his wife and focus on himself. This was foreign to him, because he had spent his whole life focused on others to orient himself, just like his wife had always done. It was also frightening in this situation because he feared that by not attending carefully to her, he risked missing opportunities to save his marriage. This was also scary for her, as she had to trust herself and her changes to stay focused on herself as he was working to do the same with himself, again vulnerable because he might get stronger and choose to leave her.

They spent a couple of years in therapy, coming every month or so, experimenting a lot with changing: her on not caving into a one-down position from which she would try to change him out of her anxiety, and him not caving into trying to determine how to please her when he was anxious about their differences. They both got much better at holding their own with each other by staying focused on Self. Their fights vanished as a problem. They still would fall into them periodically, but they could recover, realizing this was not worth the energy and was simply not necessary. He continued to bet some but it became much less of a focus in their relationship, which made it an issue of disagreement periodically, but no longer a problem. They both were very clear that they had a new connection in their relationship. Their marriage had changed for the better, and they were both very happy about that.

In spite of all these changes, Sally would have to continually monitor sliding into assumptions that she was not really that powerful or that happy. Sometimes she would have thoughts about whether she could still have done better in a husband. But her changes sustained her so she did not yield to those old assumptions. She knew her marriage was much stronger, and could acknowledge that improvement. She began to develop more open relationships with her husband's children. They were very receptive to that and saw her as a mother to them. Even though she felt good about that, she had trouble trusting herself, always saying that she was not really a mother, that she knew nothing about mothering because she had never had children of her own. Even her husband could recognize that she was much more important to his children than she realized, and he was pleased that his children could have that relationship.

Also, her business continued to grow. She hired more people and opened another store. She knew the business was becoming more and more successful, and she could enjoy that because she liked the work a lot, but it also made her nervous. She could recognize that she probably could never get rid of the vulnerability of feeling some risk of losing, the more successful she became.

Both people, Don the Magnifier and Sally the Minifier, worked to change their pattern of decision-making to move their previously stabilizing Home position closer to the Middle. Don did it by accepting the limitations of not helping his son and Sally did it by staying strong in not yielding to a one-down position with her husband and employees. While this task was difficult enough by itself for each of them to do, they were able to manage the momentum of their changes as the system responded. The systemic forces pushed Don back as his son continued to fail; as his ex-wife was critical of what he was doing; and as his administrators at school wanted him to take on more projects. The systemic forces pushed Sally back as her husband tried to engage her in the old arguments and as some of her employees expressed resentment of her changes. As each of them handled this pull of the system back to the old pattern, they were able to maintain their changes and stabilize their Home position closer to the Middle of the continuum from their respective sides. Through this long-term work of decision-making with less magnification, Don's relationship with his son and ex-wife improved significantly and he was more productive at work. Sally's long-term work of decision-making with less minification resulted in a more satisfying marriage and a more productive business. Along with the satisfaction of these positive outcomes, they also realized that they will continually feel the press to move on to more changes.

With the framework of Magnification/Minification as a process of changing the Self through changing the pattern of decision-making presented first conceptually in the earlier chapters, and now concretely in these stories, it is time to summarize the steps in the phases of change in the Guide.

Chapter 7

The Guide

Change has been the driving force for my writing this book. The Mag/Min framework has developed out of my continual experimentation with thinking and action that has led to my own changes and to those of the clients and students I work with. This book presents that framework in a self-improvement mode, but with the substantial theoretical and philosophical ideas that ground it. This chapter encapsulates the steps of the practice of changing Self, using this framework.

It condenses the ideas that have been presented so far into a two-phase guide. At first, people usually grasp the ideas quickly on an intuitive level, but then have trouble developing a clear plan about the process of how to make changes. Even as they begin to make changes, they often get lost in the flow of the changes and end up losing the overall perspective of the framework, especially with its systemic foundation. They can understand their own changes, but are surprised and confused when others in their family or workplace respond to these changes that actually affect everyone and disrupt the balance of the system. This first section of the Guide, the "Beginning Phase," provides a structure to refer to in that initial stage in which one makes changes and feels the inevitable vulnerability of operating more from the Middle. Then the second section of the Guide, the "Ongoing Phases," serves as a continual reference for living life this way from now on. The complete Guide serves an additional purpose of being a compact summary of the model.

Outline of the Guide

Beginning Phase:

Primary steps

1. Identify the Home position.
2. Identify specific behaviors that reflect current decision-making patterns.
3. Experiment with making decisions that reflect movement toward the Middle.

Ongoing Phases:

Practice tasks over the long term

❖ Using this framework as the basis for *all* decisions
❖ Understanding the other side
❖ Tolerating and learning to accept the anxiety and vulnerability that accompany this way of living.
❖ Monitoring the reductionism of Self and the loss of systems thinking

Primary Steps

1. Identify the Home position

The first step, as presented in Chapter 2, is to identify which side of the Magnification/Minification continuum one operates from. This initial step is crucial, because without knowing the Home position, a person has no way to figure out what changes to make, or to be able to assess the significance of changes they do make in the pattern of decisions and actions. Once the reader has established whether they are Mag or Min, the framework makes sense, and the book can become a personal handbook for change, not just an interesting idea.

Without knowing which way the Middle is, a person could actually make things worse by increasing the reactivity. A person whose Home position is on the Magnification side, but thinks he operates from minification, may wrongly try to take more chances and not allow limitations, increasing the reactivity of moving further toward Magnification. Similarly, a person whose Home position is on the Minification side, but thinks she operates from magnification, may decide to take less chances, moving away from the Middle on the continuum.

In the beginning, people frequently have trouble confirming the Home position. As presented in Chapter 2, this difficulty may be compounded by a difference between the operating mode of the Basic self and the Social self. If both basic and social are the same, either Mag or Min, there is less chance of confusion. However, if they are different, people have to do some extra work to clearly identify the Home position.

Having questions about alternating between sides reflects confusion about the Home position, because it has become axiomatic for me, in working with this framework for some years, that the side of the Home position never changes. When pressed far enough, with enough of a challenge as presented in Chapter 2, a firm Home position can be identified.

The clarity about the Home position provides a reliable marker for what changes to experiment with initially, and for assessing the outcome of these experiments as time goes on. This reliability is a major advantage. Now questions about what decision to make are greatly simplified. A person can trust that a particular decision is wrong for them, as it moves in the opposite direction from the Middle, either toward the Magnification or Minification ends of the continuum. A person no longer needs to vacillate. If one's Home position is Minification, any decision that is based in an ambivalence about needing to assess risk further is wrong. Any further debating about the decision is a waste of time. Similarly, a Magnifier, speculating about maybe trying to accomplish a risky endeavor, needs to simply stop thinking about it and move on. It's simple: *When in doubt, the Magnifier always needs to stop, and the Minifier always needs to go.*

In addition to this powerful simplification, which saves a great deal of mental time and affords confirming clarity, is the advantage that Home-position identification provides a way to measure change. As the experimentation proceeds, a person can evaluate a particular decision as to whether it was based in the old pattern of either magnification or minification. Then, over time the person can begin to see how the pattern may be changing.

A Minifier may notice that he trusts himself and his decisions more. He doesn't second-guess himself as much. He worries less about how he is doing, or about the outcome of some of his decisions. He also can recognize when he slips and yields to the old pattern of minification. When this happens, he knows what he needs to do then to recover, or what to do the next time. As time goes on he may hear comments from others that he seems somewhat more at ease or happier.

The Magnifier may notice she is surprisingly more relaxed, as she does not have so much on her plate. Some of the intensity of feeling driven is gone. She is surprised that, instead of feeling guilty for not doing everything, she is getting a lot done and doing it competently. People may also comment that she seems more relaxed.

As both of these people continue with their changes, they come to recognize familiar, old patterns in routine interactions with spouses, with children, and with co-workers that they can also apply to relatively unfamiliar or new decisions, such as buying a car or elective surgery. Again, the Home position serves as the reference point, the beacon through all the sorting through of options.

2. Identify specific behaviors that reflect current decision-making patterns

Behaviors indicate the pattern of decision-making that marks the Home position of either Magnification or Minification. Initially, a person uses anxiety as an important measure of where the Home position is. Minifiers are afraid of potential and Magnifiers are afraid of limitations. They begin to recognize that as they reflect on their experiences in the past or as they imagine situations that could happen in the future. They also learn the Home position by noticing behaviors that go with their pattern of decision-making, which grounds them on one side or the other of the continuum.

A Magnifier realizes that they most often will take on a challenge. They don't have to think about it. They will say "yes." That is a specific behavior for them that reveals and maintains their Home position on the Mag side of the continuum. Similarly, a Minifier notices that they most often defer or decline when presented with an opportunity to do something new. They have to think about it. They will say "maybe" or "no."

Both learn to recognize that this behavior of saying "yes" or "maybe" is evidence of their denial mode of magnification or minification. As they are regularly confronted with daily decisions to make, as well as periodic ones, that behavior will be there. Again, as the Home position is reliable as an indicator of one's stable pattern of decision-making, the specific behaviors that go with that position are equally reliable as indicators.

This is important, because it makes this framework of a denial mode very concrete in the daily lives of people. The Magnifier can recognize its operation each time they say "yes" to a challenge automatically, as can the Minifier each time they say "no" automatically.

More practically, each one can use the awareness of the pattern of that specific behavior as a concrete tool to change themself. The Magnifier can experiment with powerful changes to the Self simply by not saying "yes" to those challenges without taking some time and thinking about it. In the same way, the Minifier can experiment with saying "yes" immediately without thinking about it. This is very simple. It is not complicated with a lot of different variations to consider. And this simplicity can be trusted because of the reliability of the Home position, which does not waver from one side to the other.

It is crucial to note here that particular behaviors are not specific to either Mag or Min. While there may be some common patterns, such as Mags often being extroverts and over-achievers and Mins often being introverts and distancers, these behaviors and many others can just as well be associated with the opposite end of the continuum. The point here is that the behaviors are specific for that person and they reliably indicate that particular person's operating from magnification or minification. (See Chapter 2 and Figure 2.1 for this explanation with examples.)

3. Experiment with making decisions that reflect movement toward the Middle

In this first phase, a person has to do a lot of experimenting. People who have an immediate awareness of where the Home position is experiment to confirm their first impression, and are usually not surprised by the outcome. However, they are sometimes surprised by how pervasive the pattern is in so many areas of their life. People who are not sure at all where the Home position is, who think they operate from both sides at times, experiment to establish where the Home position really is. Like the others, they usually end up discovering that they do indeed have a Home position if they experiment enough, and then too are surprised at how consistent the patterns are around that Home position.

However, the experimentation process continues beyond the first step of identifying and confirming the Home position. Along with confirmation of the Home position, and the behaviors that manifest and embody this denial mode of Mag or Min, comes the awareness of the direction toward the Middle. Knowing which way the Middle is provides a powerful guide for change, through experimenting with different behaviors by making different decisions.

This book is about change. The framework of Magnification/Minification offers a concrete way to change the Self by modifying the patterns of one's decision-making. Behaviors reflect the patterns of decision-making. Behaviors are the bottom-line evidence of one's denial mode. People who operate from a denial mode of magnification will behave in ways that support their not having to deal with limitations. People who operate from minification will behave in ways that support their not having to deal with potential. To make changes, people experiment with making different decisions that lead to different behaviors. Minifiers try out saying "yes" instead of "maybe," then do it, and assess whether it worked out okay or whether it was a bad idea in the first place. Magnifiers see what happens when they say "no," and assess whether they indeed missed a terrific opportunity or whether it turned out okay not to do it.

Ongoing experimentation then leads to a disruption of the denial mode, as one recognizes the difference between these new behaviors and the old, predictable patterns. People who magnify begin to realize that, on balance, allowing limitations really does work out better in the long run, and people who minify realize the same thing about allowing potential. They then continue to monitor their decision-making and opt more and more to make decisions that move the Home position more toward the Middle. Of course, as they do this, their behaviors change. Mags behave in less risky ways and Mins take more risks. These behavioral changes become more stable and now reflect a different pattern. At the same time, the denial mode is different as people from each side think differently about themselves. Now the Self has changed as people act differently and think differently about who they are and why they do what they do.

As one experiments with making different decisions and behaving in different ways, thereby changing the Self, the assumption of this framework is that this change will disrupt the balance of larger systems like a family, an organization, a neighborhood, and so on. This is the case in the story of Sally in Chapter 6 and how her change of Self changed her marriage and her business. It is assumed that the Minifier operates in that way partly to maintain her part in that system. She was always putting herself down as not able to take charge of a task. The system expected that and so did she. It organized itself around that pattern, as people didn't ask her to do that much, or just the opposite; they continually harassed her to do more. With this change she had to see herself differently as others adjusted to her change. Her denial mode of minification had maintained her Self as she participated in maintaining the balance of that organization. When the Mag, whose modus operandi is always a take-charge one, experiments with not stepping up to all opportunities, people will be initially surprised, and perhaps worried about them, or disappointed, or even angry. This is the case in the story of Don in Chapter 6 and how his change of Self changed his nuclear family and his role at work. He disrupted the balance of that system, which challenged others whose Selves had been maintained by his magnifying Self. Of course, that person making the change is also challenged by the reactions of others who expect them to act in the patterned ways of the past, which in turn requires that person to deal with the change of Self they are making.

Ongoing phase

These next steps of the Guide describe the process of change over the long term, once a person has identified the Home position and the behaviors that go with it, and has experimented with decisions to the point of having made changes that have changed their behavioral patterns and thereby the Self. This is not the end of the change process because, as has been presented many times in this book, this framework is grounded in a systems model. That means that whatever happens, it is part of the balancing of systemic processes. Just as the patterns of the denial modes come from and maintain the functioning of systems like families and organizations, the very changes in those denial modes continue to be incorporated into that functioning recursively and now maintain a different functioning. So a person's changes are never independent of the larger system.

Over the long term, changes in the Basic self will carry over into a person's social interactions so that the Social self also changes. As the person changes the pattern of decision-making to shift the Home position closer to the Middle on the continuum, the awareness of the patterns of the Social self increase, and can be an additional resource as a guide for the ongoing work of change. The increased awareness of the patterns of the Social self can provide a person with validation for the changes in the Basic self as well as an alert about deviations from the new patterns.

Overall, this means that one's changes may be stable, but are never permanent. As life goes on, one will be continually challenged by events that require decisions, and the systemic patterns will press, usually in the old ways. This requires a person to continually monitor their patterns in order not to yield to the systemic pressures and regress. This second set of steps offers reminders about how to maintain one's changes of Self.

Using this framework as the basis for all decisions

As people have success in working with this framework, it can begin to be a dominant part of their lives. It begins to explain a lot. They can see how operating from their Home position makes sense out of many of their behaviors in many areas of their lives. They can understand the behaviors of others from this perspective. They can also look back into their own histories and understand better how they have developed and have made the decisions they have. They can also look back into the history of their family and understand the behavior of people they have never met.

As they have made changes based on working toward the Middle on the Mag/Min continuum, the framework becomes more validated. So it makes sense not only in understanding how they have functioned in the past, but then also in how they can continue to make changes, using it moving forward, as they proceed through the stages of the lifecycle. They find that over the long term their level of functioning improves. The problematic issues in their lives are less problematic. Magnifiers discover that, while they hate having to accept more limitation, overall they achieve more with less stress. Rather than having to accept less satisfaction in life with lower standards, their productivity is more efficient. Minifiers realize that, in spite of the anxiety of continually taking risks and saying "yes," they actually have more successes than they would have expected or think that they are capable of.

As people from both sides have this success, they begin to trust themselves more. In spite of others expecting Magnifiers to push forward every time, they are better able to trust their awareness of their own patterns, as well as the systemic dynamics of others needing them to magnify, and are able to hold to their own changed position. Likewise, Minifiers are better able to trust their own awareness that they need to take the risk and not yield to the concerns of others that they should not.

With this new and more stable awareness of Self, basically a change of Self, comes the realization that the dynamics of the Mag/Min continuum really never stop. People start to recognize that their patterns have changed but have not gone away. People who minify will always be pulled away from potential toward playing it safe, and people who magnify will always be pulled toward taking risks. This will be true in day-to-day challenges and in major life-changing events in the course of one's aging. Here is where one can see the power of this framework. It is so simple. Through all of the struggles, daily and developmental, one very efficient way to manage them all and be more effective is simply to monitor how one makes the decisions.

Rather than thinking that each new challenge presents a different set of issues and new decisions, it is much simpler to sort it out by asking which way the Middle is. Regardless of the issues, the Minifier has to find the pitfalls of yielding when that is the old pattern, and the Magnifier needs to monitor for the reflex of taking on what is wrong for them. They each need to frame the issues in terms of magnification or minification, and then proceed with how to act based on their changes.

In this way, decisions become the primary mode of monitoring for the highest level of functioning, as one trusts a Self that is more reliable. Then this begins to apply to all decisions, large and small.

However, there is a built-in catch for the power of this way of living life, which leads directly to the next step. As people from either end of the Mag/Min continuum make major changes in Self to shift the Home position more toward the Middle, the momentum never stops. People who magnify will always have to deal with more limitation and people who minify will always have to deal with more potential. The irony is that as both are more successful, productive, and higher functioning, they realize they have to continually move farther in that direction and the stakes get higher. Magnifiers have bigger limitations to handle and Minifiers have bigger potentials to accept. The momentum of their changes carries them forward and continues to press, creating more anxiety and more vulnerability, along with more calmness and productivity. I described this dynamic of the momentum of the change process both in my story and in the two composite stories in Chapter 6.

Understanding the other side

Throughout the book, the focus has been on working on Self to change the Home position, initially by identifying the side as either Magnification or Minification, learning the patterns of how one does that reflex, and then experimenting with ways to change Self in those patterns. The fundamental practice and discipline is self-focus, in which one gains orientation to others through a primary reference to oneself. This is the way the process of change in this framework operates. Of course, as one does this work, one encounters others in various systems who have different denial systems, and one learns to deal with those differences, again by monitoring Self not to yield to reactivity and fall back into one's own reflex of magnification or minification.

I often find people able to recognize their Home position, their patterns of decision-making and how it plays out in their lives, and able to make changes in those patterns, whether toward the Middle from the Minification side or from the Magnification side. But when I inquire about their understanding of people from the other side, they fall short. Minifiers still think that in some way Magnifiers are somehow better, and in their work toward the Middle they would like to be more like them. Magnifiers may reluctantly understand that they need to accept more limits in their life, but still disparage Minifiers, who may actually be more mature than they are (i.e. closer to the Middle on the continuum on the Minification side). Of course, this limited understanding of the other side reflects the fact that they have further to go with their own work toward the Middle, when the Min still limits themself by seeing the Mag as better and the Mag still sees the Min as lesser. It is another step in each of their work to move toward the Middle to be able to tolerate the vulnerability in the Middle and then to understand the other side as dealing with the same struggle, which is to allow the coexistence of potential and limitation as one makes decisions. So there is still another, important level of understanding possible.

At first as you understand the other side in your experiments with your Self, you will know the other side primarily as very different or opposite. Given the assumption that people have a Home position on only one side of the continuum and that it never changes from one side to the other, a person never has the experience of what it is like for people from the other side. People can understand the experience of the other side, but only by making the cognitive bridge in recognizing that the other's experience of anxiety in moving toward the Middle on the continuum is the same as their own. The anxiety for the Minifier in experimenting with being more powerful is the same anxiety as that for the Magnifier experimenting with accepting limits. While the anxiety is the same, because the challenge is about allowing both potential and limitation to exist side by side simultaneously, and it becomes more pronounced with movement toward the Middle, how each side experiences that same anxiety is different.

As you are able to move your Home position more toward the Middle, by definition you will be less reactive to the other side because your Self is now more stable and can respond to challenges with better adaptation. This usually takes several years. Over time, with this understanding of your own patterns, you can begin to understand the other side on its own terms. The other side is now not so oppositional, annoying, threatening, and so forth. You begin to understand the other side as dealing with the same issues of anxiety about maintaining Self in the system, but simply from the other side.

As you were beginning to make changes you learned that, as a Minifier, you no longer needed to worry about whether you were being too aggressive, powerful, dominant, and so forth. That is the right direction of change for you. Similarly, as a Magnifier, you learned that you no longer needed to worry about whether you were being too passive, weak, and so forth. That is the right direction of change for you. This understanding simplified decision-making about your own actions.

At this point, as an observer, you begin to be able to identify the Home positions of others as Magnifier or Minifier. You learn to use their behavior as an initial cue, but then are able to understand the assumptions that drive that behavior. As you can recognize others as Magnifiers or Minifiers, it helps you know how to monitor your own reactivity with them. It simplifies how you need to act in response.

The opposite Home position is usually more trouble than if the Home position is the same as yours. If you are a Magnifier, it takes extra effort to control attempts to make Minifiers do more, encourage them to take risks, be stronger, and so forth. You know you need to be more accepting of the limits of what is possible. You do not have to wonder about maybe finding better ways to push them. No. It's simple—just back off. This is self-regulation. If you are a Minifier, it takes more effort not to yield to pressure, not to seek validation for shortcomings from a Magnifier, but instead accept one's own power. You do not have to wonder about maybe finding better ways to avoid being challenged and just get along. No. It's simple—just stay strong.

When the other operates from the same Home position as you, it does not take as much effort to manage Self. While you can still get caught in reactive interactions, there is slack; there are more opportunities to self-correct. A Magnifier can see the same dynamic in another Magnifier, and from the Home position closer to the Middle on the continuum, it is easier not to go along with behavior that has a low probability of success because of ignoring limits. A Minifier can see the same dynamic in another Minifier and, again from a Home position closer to the Middle on the continuum, it is easier not to go along with behavior that sabotages the probability of success because of ignoring possibilities.

Overall, this advanced ability to understand the other side leads to more acceptance of others, as well as of oneself.

Tolerating and learning to accept the anxiety and vulnerability that accompanies this way of living

As one moves the Home position more toward the Middle, there is a change in how one approaches the world and its challenges. There is less of a hyper-vigilant scanning for any hint of limitation for Magnifiers or of potential for Minifiers. There is less of a reflex response to challenges, and more awareness that one needs to be careful in how one responds. At the same time, there is a sense that one cannot prepare ahead of time to make sure one makes the right choice about saying "no" as a Magnifier or about pursuing an opportunity as a Minifier. This way of living means being able to live more in the present, trusting one's Self in making decisions simply as events present themselves in living life.

There is some anxiety about the loss of the old, predictable pattern. While it may have been stressful and not that productive, it was reliable. It was "who I am." Now one has to make decisions that are not so automatic. The loss of that predictability leaves people feeling vulnerable. This feeling is not the same as the old anxiety about limitation or potential from the other side. It is a sense of being cut loose and on one's own in the unfamiliar territory of trusting oneself.

The benefit of living one's life with this kind of vulnerability is that one gets to make better decisions. These decisions lead to more functional behavior over the long term because they are more efficient, as people have more capacity to act on their abilities. They allow one to engage life more fully. People who magnify are able to be more productive, as they capitalize on their real strengths, because they no longer dissipate that strength by taking on too much, which ends up depleting their energy through a lot of anxiety and over functioning. People who minify are more productive, as they do not squander opportunities by repetitively avoiding possibilities for success, and can capitalize on their real strengths, better able to recognize and take advantage of opportunities that may break through.

Becker says it takes courage to allow the vulnerability that occurs in the Middle, where life is more productive. He says people do not have the "strength to bear the superlative" (Becker, p. 49).

Monitoring the reductionism of Self and the loss of systems thinking

One does not get to change the Home position permanently. The change is to a point closer to the Middle on the continuum, around which one's basis for making decisions is significantly different, different enough that the pattern changes. But it does not mean that a Mag never makes the old decision at times and opts to take on more than they should, just as the Min does reject bona fide opportunities at times.

As stated in the previous step of allowing vulnerability, at times it is just too much and people yield to the old pattern. Sometimes they are aware of what they are doing. "I don't care, I'm just going to do it this time." Sometimes they only realize it afterward. "I just did it again." Usually some challenge provokes enough anxiety that the old pattern kicks in.

Generally this regressive thinking about the decision reflects the old reductionism about the Self as an individual, with a loss of systems thinking. It is often the anxiety in the system that presses the person back into the old pattern. The Mag yields to the old sense of Self as a go-getter, a doer, a successful make-it-happen person, ignoring how this identity is embedded in the systemic patterns from the family, workplace, or whatever system they are dealing with. Similarly, the Min defaults to the old Self as a quiet, shy, not powerful, non-aggressive person, ignoring how this identity is embedded in the systemic patterns from the family, workplace, or whatever system they are dealing with. Others expect the person to go back and be "who they were," often because they themselves need the person to be that old way.

But even with regression and mistakes, all is never lost. It is always possible to recover. This is precisely why the Mag/Min framework is so powerful. Because it is based in systems theory, this means that as systems are always in motion and maintaining a balance, one gets the chance to recover the next time around. The momentum continues and gives the person second chances. Sometimes that means changing the decision immediately. "Sorry, I just changed my mind." Or sometimes the decision can be reversed later on: "You know, after thinking about that decision awhile, I realized it is not what I want to do." Or sometimes, you cannot reverse that decision, but get to make a different decision the next time about that same issue. "I'm not going to make that same mistake this time."

As the reader can see, the first three steps that comprise the Beginning phase are basically sequential, where one accomplishment builds on the previous one. The Ongoing phases consist of challenges to maintaining the changes achieved in the Beginning phase. This Guide then functions as a comprehensive summary of the framework seen as a whole. The reader can refer to it initially to gain a better understanding of the framework and how to use it, as well as, over the long term, to remember the basic operations as they make changes and face new challenges to the Self.

Conclusion

Back to where this book began

This is an important book for you and for me. For readers, it makes a significant contribution as a framework and a tool for people to make better decisions for themselves in their own lives, as well as for the lives of others, be they parents, supervisors, politicians, or others in positions of responsibility.

What makes it so significant? As I have said from the beginning and throughout this book, the framework of Magnification/Minification is powerful. It is powerful just as an idea. People quickly get the sense that it encapsulates some important dimensions of the human condition, not in a simplistic or ideological way, but in a way that connects deep and complex factors about life and death. Exploration of the framework and experimentation with the change of Self leads to a fuller understanding of the human experience of being alive, as it provides access to the richness of these connections.

The framework is also powerful because it is more than an idea. It is a very practical way to make changes in how one lives one's life. A person can use it as a guide for making important decisions that have major impacts. It also helps a person change the pattern of decision-making with many smaller decisions that end up changing the Self. And, the changing of the Self can produce changes in relationships in a family or an organization that leverage the power of the framework to extend beyond just an idea or a guide for one person. For a leader in an organization with significant power, like the head of a company or a political leader, the power of the framework extends even further into larger networks.

Research in neuroscience may validate the power of this framework from science if it confirms my hypothesis from experience that the Home position reflects a brain reflex, and that the different sides of the continuum of Magnification and Minification reflect different brain patterns, not personality types. Then changing the Home position is a change in brain patterns.

For me, this book is a powerful accomplishment as a Minifier, a concrete manifestation of my legacy for future generations, as a parent for my children, and as a therapist and teacher for my clients and students.

However, there is a problem. As I see it, there are two counter factors that can undermine the power of the framework. One is at the level of the individual and the other is at the level of the culture. Both are a problem of other-focus. At the level of the individual, a major problem is the one I addressed in the Guide, of people not being able to understand others who operate from the other side of the continuum. It is possible to gain a significant understanding of Mag and Min as an idea and use it productively in one's life, but still not be able to use its full power to change systems. That is one inhibiting factor.

The other problem is the cultural preference for magnification. Generally, Western culture values potential as strong and sees limitation as weak. This can be seen in the polarization of the notion of optimism and pessimism. No one thinks that pessimism is a good outlook. For the Mag/Min framework, if one operates from the Minification side, fairly close to the Middle as a very mature person, the Magnifier who is much less mature, farther out on the continuum from that side, will still be seen as having a better, more positive attitude toward life, in spite of that person's basic immaturity.

This strong cultural preference for potential inhibits the power of the Mag/Min framework, because it prevents people from distinguishing maturity, and the work toward it, from an attitude about life, extreme magnification, that is basically an avoidance of the anxiety about life and death, an avoidance of potential and limitation side by side.

What can be done to overcome these two factors of not understanding the other side and of valuing potential over limitation, each of which inhibits the power of this framework? It basically comes down to the same thing. Everyone, from either side, needs to operate more from a primary position of self-focus to move closer to the Middle, and not let oneself be determined by a focus on the other, which should be secondary. To see the other side through one's own reactive position (Minifiers seeing Mags as better and Magnifiers seeing Mins as lesser) reflects the inability of both of them to tolerate the anxiety of moving farther toward the Middle. For the Minifier to view the Magnifier as stronger, better, and so forth, is actually yielding to the old pattern of minifying, and for the Magnifier to view the Minifier as weaker, lesser, and so forth in the very same way is yielding to the old pattern of magnification.

So this is a problem of using the framework to make changes up to a certain point and then stopping, no longer continuing to experiment and allow more anxiety. Most likely what happens is that the momentum of their changes creates enough anxiety that people need to manage the vulnerability and restrict further momentum. The Magnifiers fear the power of more limitations as they see the Minifiers successful, and the Minifiers fear the power of more potential as they see the Magnifiers successful. The power of the framework is there, if people can take advantage of it. It does not have to be limited in this way.

So, the framework can be most powerful when people can understand their own Home position and from there understand how people operate from the other side. It is not an experience of walking in the other's shoes and knowing what it is like. Rather, it is understanding what the other side must be like through the common experience of anxiety, using the framework to make sense of how that other person thinks and acts, particularly in relation to you.

With this understanding of both sides, individual people can resist the second inhibiting factor of the cultural assumptions of valuing potential, as the Magnifer does not take this assumption as validation of their own Home position and the Minifier does not take it as criticism of theirs. Given that this framework provides people with a way to change and be more effective in their lives, people from both sides, understanding the cultural reactivity about potential, can be stronger in the larger systems of society, in their systems of families, organizations, and so forth, to act on that understanding and thereby change those larger systems. So again, the leverage for change is with individual people changing Self in their systems and moving toward the center of the Mag/Min continuum.

The whole process of writing this book has been a powerful experience for me. In order to write it I had to recognize how much this idea has changed me. My life is clearly different in many ways: a powerful Minifier, but still a Minifer. I am a long way from the depression of my early years in high school and college, and from the anger in the relationship with my mother. My relationships in my nuclear family with my wife and my sons are much stronger and better balanced. In my professional life I am so much more comfortable and confident in what I know and in operating as a teacher and a leader. I can also recognize how much my work as a therapist and teacher has impacted the lives of others in very important and positive ways. The stronger I am the more I realize how much people care about me. I can accept that love much more than I could before when I would discount their valuing me because I did not value myself as much.

That is all evidence of major changes in my Self. However, it is abundantly clear to me that I am still a Minifier. I am always aware of it. But, as the track of my decisions on the chart (Figure 6.2) shows, my Home position is unmistakably closer to the Middle, which is what accounts for these significant changes.

However, I still get anxious about my potential and being powerful. Ironically, my changes to acknowledge and accept that I am smart, a good therapist and a good teacher (a major challenge for a Minifier) sometimes lead to the opposite problem of thinking I am better than others. I can become judgmental about people who do not agree with me. My Social mag becomes more prominent and overshadows my Basic min. The corrective, counter-balancing thought for me in that situation is always to remember that I stand on the shoulders of people who have come before me and whose work I have drawn from. I remind myself that the creation of this Mag/Min framework is not all mine. This is a real limitation, not a distorted one of minification. But at the same time this acknowledgement does not at all negate the power of what I have created from knowledge passed on to me. This is again Becker's Existential Paradox: I am unique and I am common, both at the same time.

Earlier in my life I would discount the strength and significance of my thinking, which sabotaged the momentum of the ideas flowing from the work of scholars and researchers through me to future generations. Now to make the mistake of hubris or arrogance and think these ideas are mine, also blocks that flow as I interact with others from my Social mag.

Hubris is my attempt to protect the gains of acceptance of my potential by diminishing the limitation of people disagreeing with me. This makes me less vulnerable as I interact from my Social mag, because internally I minify the depth of my thinking by not trusting it as strong, and therefore need to protect my ideas.

A good example of this is my surprise in learning over the years that as I have made presentations in my classes and at meetings with colleagues, people would get very interested and excited when I would share personal material. As a Minifier, I would wonder why they would care about the foibles of my particular life. Then, as I did the work to accept my potential and realized how important my ideas were, I worry that sharing too much personal material would jeopardize the strength of those ideas as people began to see my inadequacies.

The work is still for me to control the minification of my Basic self, which makes it easier to control the reactivity of my Social mag as I allow myself to be vulnerable. I now share more personal information about myself as I make presentations. A major example of that is my personal story in this book. In this way the ideas are potent; I am powerful *and* humble, unique *and* common; and the flow of knowledge is not impeded.

So this book is powerful as I pass on these ideas and present them as my contribution to a larger audience than the relatively small world of my family, my clients, students, supervisees, and colleagues. I have worked hard to distill the ideas I have drawn from others, and to present them in an integrated and coherent way that makes them available to many other people. That is why I care so much about the ideas being distorted by individuals or cultures as mentioned above; it disrupts the momentum of this generational flow of knowledge for everyone.

———————

In closing, I will say that, as a Minifier, writing this book and claiming the power of the framework is a major step in my moving closer to the Middle on the continuum, and in making this contribution to the world, as I present it now to you, my readers.

I wish you, both Magnifiers and Minifiers, the same success in using the framework to become a better self and make your own contribution to our world. That can be powerful indeed.

Frequently Asked Questions

The Two *Most* Frequently Asked Questions

1. Can't you be both a Magnifier and a Minifier? Couldn't a person operate sometimes from one side of the continuum as a Magnifier and at other times from the other side as a Minifier, for example, one way at work and another at home?

No. There are three reasons for confusion about this question of being both.

1.) While Magnification is on one side of the continuum and Minification is on the other side, it is still one continuum of the same perceptual reflex about the probability of a favorable or unfavorable outcome, with more distortion at either end and less distortion as the Home position is closer to the Middle. For both it is the same reflex to focus on the likely outcome, but with a directly opposite perception from each side: for the Magnifier the favorable outcome is figural with unfavorable in the background, and for the Minifier the unfavorable outcome is figural with favorable in the background. This figure/ground set stays the same because it is a primitive reaction a person cannot change. However, a person can change the response to the reflex, but that is a move toward the Middle from the Home position side, not a flip to the different reflex on the other side.

2.) When the Home position is closer to the Middle from either side, the distortion is less pronounced and the difference between the two reflexes may be difficult to discern. However, the similarity comes from being closer to the Middle from either side, not from being on both sides. It may take some time and self-examination to determine the figural assumption of the Basic self, but knowing that it must be one or the other helps one experiment with which one it is, rather than trying to understand how it is both.

3.) The Home position is determined by the Basic self. If, however, the Social self is the opposite, it can create confusion as the person attempts to identify the Home position, because they may think they operate from both sides depending on different situations. This is a common source of uncertainty as the person initially works to identify their Home position, but sorting out the Social self usually resolves the confusion.

See: Chapters 1, 2

2. What's wrong with using the simple polarity of "maximize-minimize," instead of creating the strange word "minify"?

"Minify" is a real word which the dictionary defines simply as the opposite of "magnify." The reason for using it, rather than "minimize," is an important one for the understanding of the whole framework. Magnify and Minify are two poles of a continuum of distortions with the least distortion in the Middle. The words "maximize" and "minimize" do not convey any sense of distortion. An additional problem is that they do convey values of one over the other, where maximize is generally assumed to be better than minimize in regard to human functioning. In contrast, magnification and minification are equally dysfunctional as distortions.

See: Introduction

Magnifiers and Minifiers —

Similarities and Differences

3.1 Aren't most Magnifiers: driven, overachieving, overbearing, impatient, always knowing the answer? (Usually said by Minifiers; the list goes on and on.)

3.2 Aren't most Minifiers: passive, underachieving, dependent, indecisive? (Usually said by Magnifiers; the list goes on and on.)

These strong negative characteristics do describe a difference between the people with the Mag reflex and those with the Min reflex. However, they depict different sides of the same coin, namely, the distance from the Middle on the continuum to either end. If the distance is the same and extreme, overachieving and underachieving for example, are equally dysfunctional. Closer to the Middle these two characteristics reflect different styles of approaching tasks and may not be dysfunctional at all.

Also, the stronger emotionally charged, negative attributions about the opposite reflex usually reflect a more extreme Home position for the person making the statements. At the same time, this also reflects a limited understanding of the framework, not taking into account how the basic dynamics of distortion about the favorable or unfavorable outcomes function in the same way on both sides of the continuum.

See: Conclusion

3.3 Once you understand magnification and minification, and have recognized yourself as a Magnifier or Minifier, isn't it relatively easy to identify others as Mag or Min by observing their behavior?

No. While it is a possible to make some good guesses that may be accurate, it is actually very difficult. This is because the same behavior may indicate a Mag or a Min, just as opposite behaviors may indicate the same pattern of magnification or minification. The Home position is the position of the Basic self, which is based on the person's assumption about the possibility of a favorable outcome for their decisions. When observing a person's behavior, it is difficult to know whether that behavior is more a function of the Basic self or the Social self, because a person can have a Basic self that is the same as the Social self (MAG/mag or MIN/min) or a Basic self that is different (MAG/min or MIN/mag). The other complication is the Whole/Details dynamic in which the Magnifier and the Minifier will behave in the same way but from the opposite perception of what is figural, the whole or the details. The only way to make an accurate assessment of whether a person is a Magnifier or a Minifier is to identify the Basic self, which requires discovering the fundamental assumptions about favorable or unfavorable outcomes behind the behaviors one observes.

See: Chapters 2, 5, 7

3.4. Isn't it a problem if the Basic self and the Social self are opposite, because they should be consistent; or isn't it a problem if the Basic and Social selves are the same because there should be a balance?

Neither of these situations is a problem, because there is a complex and stable coordination between the Basic and Social selves, whether the coordination is between them as the same or as opposite. The Social self operates in tandem with the Basic self as people interact all the time in their daily lives. For some people (MAG/mag and MIN/min) these social interactions mirror the assumption about the probability of a favorable outcome for their decisions as too high (MAG) or too low (MIN). They will act socially with the same assumptions. For others (MAG/min and MIN/mag) their social interactions will reflect the opposite assumptions about the probability of a favorable outcome for their decisions. The MAG/min will act socially *as if* the probability is low when internally their Basic self still assumes it to be higher than they act like it is. Similarly, the MIN/mag will act socially *as if* the probability is high when internally their Basic self still assumes it to be lower than they act like it is.

The attention should not be on whether the Social self is the same or opposite of the Basic self, but on the assumptions about the probability of a favorable outcome for one's decisions from the Basic self. Changes in the Social self will follow from changes in the Basic, whichever the Social is for that person, the same or opposite.

See: Chapters 2, 5, 7

4. Isn't it harder for Mags to deal with Mins and for Mins to deal with Mags, compared to dealing with people with the same reflex as you?

Yes. This is because of the way the reflex works. Mags focus on the probability of a favorable outcome and block out the probability of an unfavorable outcome, which is precisely what Mins evoke with their focus on the probability of an unfavorable outcome. And of course it works the same way in the opposite situation, where Mags evoke just what Mins block out, which is the probability of a favorable outcome.

So the challenge for Mags is to control their reactivity with Mins, with behaviors like slowing down, being more patient, allowing ambiguity, and so forth. For Mins the challenge in dealing with Mags is to be more careful, clear, and decisive. This extra effort with the opposite reflex is not a matter of being phony. It is actually the work that the person, Mag or Min, needs to do anyway to move closer to the Middle. It is just that dealing with the opposite reflex in another person highlights that challenge. The more extreme the Home positions, the more effort it takes. The closer to the Middle, the less the challenge, because the person is already better at regulating Self in the face of the opposite reflex.

When dealing with another person with the same reflex, the challenge is not to join with that person in protecting the Self from the anxiety about moving toward the Middle. This means that Mins need to monitor their reactivity and not go along with another Min about the Likelihood of an unfavorable outcome, ignoring the realistic probability of a favorable outcome. And Mags need to monitor their reactivity and not go along with another Mag about the Likelihood of a favorable outcome, ignoring the realistic probability of an unfavorable outcome.

See: Chapter 7

5. So then, Magnifiers focus only on the Probability of a Favorable Outcome and Minifiers only on an Unfavorable one?

This is accurate, but only half of the dynamic. The other half is that Magnifiers block out the probability of an unfavorable outcome, and Minifiers block out the probability of a favorable outcome. The two foci operate simultaneously as a synchronized unit of perception. This creates a complete and immediate perception, comprised of both figure and ground, that organizes the challenging input so a person grasps the situation and can act. For a Magnifier who assesses the probability as very favorable, having to allow concerns that it may not be that promising disrupts that perception. The probability of a favorable outcome remains in the foreground (figural) and the probability of an unfavorable outcome stays in the background (ground), forming the complete perception. In the same way for the

Minifier, the probability of an unfavorable outcome remains in the foreground (figural) and the probability of a favorable outcome stays in the background (ground), forming the complete perception. So for Magnifiers an essential part of seeing the probability as mostly favorable requires simultaneously excluding the problem of it not being so positive. In the same way for Minifiers, the possibility that a decision will lead to a favorable outcome disrupts the perception that it will not, and therefore stays simultaneously in the background.

See: Introduction

6. Is it true that Magnifiers have a good self-concept and Minifiers have a poor self-concept?

No. Magnifier/Minifier identifies the pattern of decision-making for a person that defines their Self. Self-concept is a psychological term that defines how a person feels about their basic worth. To demonstrate the divergence between these two ideas, it is possible for a less mature Magnifier to have a poor sense of their worth as a person while continuing to ignore the possibilities of unfavorable outcomes, continuing to make bad decisions, and then feel reinforced as not worth much. In contrast, it is possible for a more mature Minifier to continue to ignore some possibilities for favorable outcomes, but feel comfortable and satisfied about their worth.

See: Introduction

7. Isn't it still better to be a Magnifier than a Minifier?

No. Magnification is just as much a distortion, a protection from anxiety, as minification. At the extremes it is just as rigid a self-protection process as minification. However, this is a valid question because Western cultures tend to support magnification over minification.

A Magnifier may derive a lot of validation for their behavior from this cultural bias. The more other-focused a person is, the farther the Home position is from the Middle and the less mature the person is. The fact that the cultural validation does not accurately reflect their strength may not be apparent to them or to others reacting to them. With a Home position closer to the Middle, the person recognizes that their real strength comes from their acceptance of limitation, which the culture does not support.

A Minifier may experience invalidation by the culture. The more other-focused a person is, the farther the Home position is from the Middle and the less mature the person is. The fact that their invalidation does not reflect weakness may not be apparent to them or to others reacting to them. With a Home position closer to the Middle, the person recognizes that their strength comes more from their acceptance of potential which the culture does support, but not to the exclusion of limitation which the culture does not support.

See: Conclusion

8. Aren't Magnifiers actually more successful in the world?

Sometimes, yes. The reason for this success is not because the magnification reflex is fundamentally more functional or productive, but because the culture supports and rewards this distortion. One could argue that this distortion on a societal level leads to the same inflexibility on that level as on the individual level, for example with dictatorships, oppressive regimes, cults, and so forth.

See: Conclusion

9. Isn't it true that men tend to be Magnifiers and women tend to be Minifiers?

No. There is no simple correlation of gender with either Magnification or Minification. This question usually stems from the cultural differences where men are disproportionally in positions of power compared to women, and people in power are often Magnifiers. Women in positions of power are just as likely to be Magnifiers, but there are fewer of them.

See: Examples throughout of Magnifiers and Minifiers from both genders

Nature of this framework

10. Isn't this Magnifier/Minifier idea just another personality scheme?

No. Identifying a person as a Magnifier or a Minifier names their pattern of decision-making. It occurs as people operate in systems. It does not depict a particular, individual, psychological profile of their emotional functioning, but rather a universal phenomenon of reacting to challenges in living. This framework first identifies which reflex the person has, and then provides scaling for how extreme that pattern is. Next, unlike a personality profile approach, the framework provides a way to change the pattern, not to modify characteristics of the person's nature. A move to a more mature Home position closer to the Middle changes the person's level of functioning, not who they are.

See: Introduction, Chapters 3, 5

11. So this framework is basically about making better decisions, based on assessing probabilities? It sounds like a manual for developing strategies for better outcomes.

It is about making better decisions, but it is about much more than that. It is about making better decisions that change the Self. At the extreme ends of the continuum, people make decisions that distort a good assessment of the probability of favorable or unfavorable outcomes, but the reason for that distortion is anxiety. It is a poor assessment process because of emotional factors. People can change the Self as they experiment with making decisions based on a better assessment of what is possible and not possible, but this requires handling that anxiety in a more mature way. So rather than being a strategy for dealing with the external world, changing the pattern of decision-making changes the Self internally. One could think of this book as a manual, not for self-improvement strategies, but as a guide for developing a practice in living.

See: Introduction, Chapters 3, 5, 7

12. How is this framework any different from the many self-improvement books out there?

The difference is systems. This framework is based in systems theory. That essentially means that the Self is not autonomous. The Self is embedded in sets of relationships that maintain themselves with a balance that provides stability for the system as a whole and for the individuals that comprise it. Family, both nuclear and extended, is the primary system for a person's maintenance of Self because of the genetic and emotional connections, but the same dynamics also occur in other social systems such as organizations, neighborhoods, communities, and so forth.

Therefore, a person's decision-making patterns and Home position are part of maintaining their own stability in the systems they live in, and any changes in Self change the balance of those systems. This is very different from a self-improvement method that assumes a person is an autonomous individual and their changes can be made independently without changing others.

See: Chapters 2, 4, 5, 6

13. Okay, so this framework is different because of its foundation in systems theory, but what difference does that make, really?

This framework differs radically from conventional thinking about the Self. Most approaches for the Self are based in individual thinking that assumes the Self is autonomous. If some other approaches do consider the Self in the context of systems, they separate out the Self as an individual part of the system. The Mag/Min framework assumes that the Self is integral with the systems it functions in, so that the system creates and maintains the Selves of the people in it, as each person contributes to the maintenance of the balance of the system as they maintain their Selves.

This conceptual difference from conventional thinking makes for a very different way of living life using this framework. It basically requires a focus on Self as primary, versus an other-focus. With self-focus, the person orients themselves through an understanding of the dynamics and patterns of the systems they live in. With the other-focus from conventional thinking, a person understands their world in terms of what is going on outside of one's own behaviors which affects the Self, rather than seeing how one's own behaviors affect others and then how those responses affect their Self in an ongoing recursion.

The Magnifier maintains orientation and self-focus as they recognize that they get in trouble if they forget their tendency to ignore limitations when challenged by the external environment. The Minifier maintains orientation and self-focus as they recognize that they get in trouble if they forget their tendency to ignore potential when challenged by the external environment.

That mode of Self-focus serves as the basis for working to change the Self, as a person experiments from either side with making different decisions in the work of moving the Home position toward the Middle of the continuum.

See: Chapters 3, 4

14. Once you grasp this framework, it is very intuitive and easy to understand, but a.) not that difficult to implement (Magnifier), or b.) very difficult to implement (Minifier)?

Magnifiers and Minifiers will react very differently to the very idea of this framework, based precisely on each of their opposite reflexes. The framework is built on the idea that a person's Self and its stability is critical to being able to survive and function in the world. The Self must be able to manage the physical threats to staying alive, but also the psychological threats to its well-being. This is an issue of the fundamental anxiety of existence, existential anxiety. This framework posits two different and opposite ways to do this, protecting the Self from this anxiety: magnification and minification. The very framework challenges Magnifiers and Minifiers precisely in these opposite ways. Magnifiers will react to this whole framework as a limitation of their potential (for example, just being defined on only one side of the continuum), and will handle this challenge by considering the framework as not that significant or the work as not that difficult. Minifiers will react to this whole framework as validation of their struggle to achieve potential (for example, just being identified as a "Minifier"), and will handle this challenge by considering the framework as accurate and the work as a life-long effort with limited results.

As both are able to move the Home position more toward the Middle on the continuum, they understand the overall framework in more depth, not just from their side of the continuum.

See: Chapter 7

15. Why is this book full of redundancies in always stating the particular topic for a Magnifier and then repeating it again for the Minifier, but just with the opposite wording?

It is crucial to state the topic for each side in its own terms precisely because of the reactivity of people not understanding the reflex of the opposite side until they first get to understand their own reflex and patterns. Only then can they understand the opposite reflex as the same but with just the opposite dynamic. So initially Magnifiers can understand magnification on its own from their lived experience, but only later can they understand minification by extrapolating from a logical explanation of it, thinking of it as magnification in reverse.

And then (to demonstrate this exact point here), Minifiers can understand minification on its own from their lived experience, but only later can they understand magnification by extrapolating from a logical explanation of it, thinking of it as minification in reverse.

See: Conclusion

16. Isn't this just another therapist's ideas about how to help people based on what has worked in his practice?

It certainly does come from my experience of over 40 years of practice as a therapist, but it has a much broader foundation, because it also comes from my experience as a college professor. My courses require the study of systems theory, neuroscience, language, and psychotherapy. Over the years, I have read a great deal and learned a great deal from the study of these fields. In addition, through this learning, I have been able to understand the powerful, common ideas that intersect these fields, and have been able to synthesize them into this basic framework of Magnification/Minification. So it is a culmination of my life's work, in a broad and expansive way that allows further development by the next generations, rather than a prescriptive outline that narrows the focus to follow the framework in a set way based on my experience.

Also, this framework, based on the integration of these ideas from many great thinkers, has been tested both in my classroom as students have engaged these ideas and challenged me, as well as in my office with my clients who have worked with these ideas to improve their lives and shown me how the framework works.

See: Introduction

Change

17. Isn't it better to have a balance between magnification and minification so the Home position is closer to the Middle?

No. This is a misunderstanding of the continuum. The Home position is always on one side or the other. People can change their pattern of decision-making and move the Home position closer to the Middle by working to control the reflex that is automatic and primary for them (either magnification or minification) and defines the Basic self, but not by adopting the opposite distortion to balance out the primary distortion. As a person can control this reflex, one can assess the probability of a favorable or unfavorable outcome with less distortion, which is how one moves the Home position closer to the Middle, where there is less distortion.

See: Chapters 1, 2

18. How do I precisely identify just where my Home position is on the scale of the continuum?

It is not possible to determine exact points on the continuum, because it is not designed as a measuring instrument. It is more of a graphic image to portray the concept of the reflexes of magnification and minification as being opposite manifestations of the same dynamic of managing the anxiety of the probabilities of a favorable or unfavorable outcome simultaneously. In addition to depicting the two opposite sides, the continuum allows for identifying in a general way how far away the Home position is from the Middle, more like "a little" or "a lot."

See: Chapter 2

19. Are words really enough to shift the Home position?

Yes. Language is a crucial component of the foundation of this framework. Language is how we make sense of the world and how we interact with others so that we all contribute to the creation of a shared sense of reality. An essential dimension of this process of maintaining reality is the stability of the Self, which happens through the process of memory in the brain. We remember who we are; others remember who we are; and we remember who they are. This memory is sequential, as it forms a narrative, a story, a person's biography. Language is the underlying process for all of this. It is important to remember that language is not just a process of the spoken word, but of thinking as well.

Thus, when a Magnifier makes a decision to act differently, for example to experiment with allowing limitation, or a Minifier to allow potential, it takes language to make that happen, as the person thinks about doing it; as they reflect on it after doing it; as they talk with others about doing it; as others think about their doing it, and talk with them about doing it. As this experimenting goes on using language, the person can change the pattern of decision-making and thereby move the Home position, which is a change of Self to a different point of stability.

See: Chapter 5

20. Don't you need a therapist to work with this framework?

It is true that I developed this framework out of my practice as a therapist and I continue to develop it, along with many of the therapists I have taught and trained who also work with this framework. So it is very helpful to work with a therapist, especially one who understands this framework, but I don't see this as a requirement. It is also possible for a person to understand this framework and work with a therapist who is not familiar with it, integrating their work of changing Self through changing the pattern of decision-making in psychotherapy with a therapist whose approach is compatible.

See: Chapter 3

Appendix

This framework of Magnification/Minification is built on the foundation of three major thinkers and writers, and on my integration of their work.

Murray Bowen

Murray Bowen created Bowen theory, which is a systems theory of human behavior in which humans function as living systems in the rest of nature, not as some psychological entities that exist apart from the natural world. Bowen theory is the basis for the idea that is the core construct in the framework: the Self.

Ernest Becker

Ernest Becker was a psychoanalytic anthropologist who developed the idea of the existential paradox, in which the human is simultaneously aware of being able to imagine themselves as eternal while knowing that they will die. He postulated that the intensity and terror of this unresolvable conflict require "denial" in order to live a sane life. His existential paradox is the basis for the continuum, with Magnification on one end and Minification on the other. This paradox is the same dynamic as what happens with my Middle position as a person makes decisions based on the simultaneous consideration that the outcome will be favorable or unfavorable. One cannot continue to consider both at once and so denies the other side in order to maintain sanity.

Humberto Maturana

Humberto Maturana is a Chilean biologist who developed a theory of living systems in which they function as "autopoietic" systems. This means that what systems do is constantly operate to maintain their integrity (organization) and stay alive, and they do this, continually create themselves over and over (auto=self; poiein=make), precisely by interacting in the environment of other systems, not autonomously. The part I take from Maturana is his conceptualization of the human as staying alive and continuously creating itself through language. For Maturana, language is a physiological process of survival, not an additional component of human beings' ability to communicate. Magnify/Minify is wholly a process of language. Change happens as a person uses language to change the Self.

Bowen—Becker—Maturana

As comprehensive and profound as the work of each of these three thinkers is, there are parts that are missing for me in each one, but I have discovered those missing parts in the others. This discovery has led to my integration of them into a complex and powerful whole which transcends each of them individually and has become the foundation for Magnification/Minification.

Bowen's conceptualization of the human as a living system that functions in accordance with the laws of nature is ground-breaking and has become a powerful theory. However, in spite of the central importance of anxiety in his theory, he never relates to the anxiety of survival in the natural world as experienced by the human, which Becker captures in his Existential Paradox. Also, Bowen does not incorporate language as a critical component of human interaction, whereas this is the core of Maturana's theory about the human as a natural system.

Becker's basic theory was psychoanalytic, a framework of individual functioning, not a systems one like Bowen's and not one based in the human as a natural living system, in spite of Becker's acute focus on the human as mortal. In addition, Becker does not relate to language as a function of human interaction.

Maturana's is a systems theory of the human as a natural living system, embedded in the process of language as autopoetic, but Maturana does not relate to the existential anxiety created by the human's awareness of mortality made possible precisely through language.

Of course, these omissions in no way represent a criticism of the work of any of them. It is because of their creative and pioneering work that I have been able to build on it and create this framework as I integrate theirs. I stand on their shoulders.

Gestalt

I have also drawn from Gestalt theory for the conceptualization of Figure/Ground in which the perception of the probabilities of a favorable or unfavorable outcome are linked in opposite ways for the Magnifier and the Minifier. Favorable is figural for the Magnifier and unfavorable is figural for the Minifier.

Neuroscience

Finally, the world of neuroscience has exploded in recent years with the benefit of computers that can scan the brain in real time so that researchers can see what is happening in the brain. Bowen, Becker, and Maturana did not have this resource when they were developing their theories. This research can provide support for my integration of my core three writers, as I propose that Magnify/Minify is a reflex, a brain function.

There are four neuroscientists whose work relates to this foundational integration. **Joseph LeDoux** (LeDoux, 2002) and **Antonio Damasio** (Damasio, 2010) both focus on the brain and the Self. LeDoux is interested in how the brain functions so that we have an awareness of being conscious, of having a Self. He focuses on memory, so that one can say that we have a Self because we can remember who we are. Damasio is interested in the brain as part of the whole body, and how the hierarchical emotional system of feedback to the brain eventually leads to consciousness and the thought of being a Self.

While their work about the Self is very important to me and my integration of magnification/minification as a brain process, it does not focus on the brain in relationship to other brains in interpersonal relationships. **Terrence Deacon** (Deacon, 1997) and **Daniel Siegel** (Siegel, 1999) do incorporate this social dimension.

Deacon's work is about the human brain as it has evolved from other forms of life, and he ends up postulating that the human brain has evolved to be the large size that it is because humans needed to be able to do language in order to survive. Humans need to interact with other humans to survive and they need language to be able to do that.

Siegel's work is focused on the impact of humans' brains on each other as they interact in relationships over time, particularly as brains grow and develop from infancy in interaction with parents. Brains change each other and end up in stable patterns.

The reader can see how this neuroscience research relates to the major ideas in my framework that I integrated from Bowen, Becker, and Maturana, namely the Self, systems, interpersonal relationships, language, and survival.

References

Becker, E. (1973). *Denial of death.* New York: Macmillan.

Bowen, M. (1978). *Family therapy in clinical practice.* New York: Jason Aronson, Inc.

Cannon, W. (1932). *Wisdom of the body.* New York: Norton.

Capra, F. (1996). *The web of life.* New York: Doubleday.

Damasio, A. (2010). *Self comes to mind.* New York: Pantheon.

Deacon, T. (1997). *The symbolic species.* New York: Norton.

Donne, J. (1975). *Devotions upon emergent occasions (A. Raspa, Ed.).* Montreal: McGill-Queen's University Press. (Original work published 1624).

Kerr, M. E., & Bowen, M. (1988). *Family evaluation: An approach based on Bowen theory.* New York: W.W. Norton.

Kohler, W. (1947). *Gestalt psychology.* New York: Liveright.

LeDoux, J. (2002). *The synaptic self.* New York: Penguin.

Maturana, H. R., & Varela, F. J. (1972). *Autopoesis and cognition.* Dordrecht, Holland: D. Reidel.

Maturana, H. R., & Varela, F. J. (1987). *The tree of knowledge.* Boston: Shambhala.

Oxford English Dictionnary. (2010). Oxford University Press.

Pind, J. L. (2013). *Edgar Rubin and psychology in Denmark: Figure and Ground.* Switzerland: Springer International Publishing.

Siegel, D. J. (1999). *The developing mind.* New York: Guilford.

Index

self-focus, 225
   change, 71
Siegel, Daniel, 19, 143
stories
   author's, 157
   composites, 193
   Mary and Paul, 23
systems theory
   balance, 69
   change in family system, 177
   self and other focus, 70

T

Tree of Knowledge, 137
triangles
   change of self, 129
   level of functioning, 111
   mag and min configurations, 114
   mixed mag and min, 124
   neutrality, 113
   self/other-focus, 108
   three mags, 114
   three mins, 119
triangles (concept)

Bowen theory, 105
   definition, 105

U

understanding other side
   as step in guide, 216

V

Varela, Francisco, 136
vulnerability
   as step in guide, 219
   long term change, 192
   Middle, 36

W

Web of Life, 139
work
   change long term, 153
   difficult, 12
   multigenerational, 167
   practice, 91
   to change, 9

32047589R00157

Made in the USA
Middletown, DE
21 May 2016